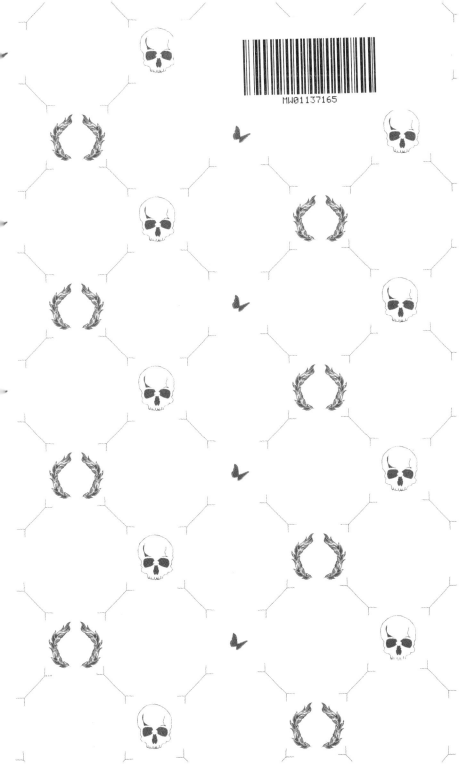

Remember Your Death

MEMENTO MORI

Lenten Devotional

By Theresa Aletheia Noble, FSP

Pauline
BOOKS & MEDIA

Library of Congress Cataloging-in-Publication Data

Names: Noble, Theresa, author.

Title: Remember your death : Memento mori Lenten devotional / by Theresa Aletheia Noble, FSP.

Description: Boston, MA : Pauline Books & Media, 2019.

Identifiers: LCCN 2018036691| ISBN 9780819865175 (pbk.) | ISBN 0819865176 (pbk.)

Subjects: LCSH: Death--Religious aspects--Catholic Church--Prayers and devotions. | Lent--Prayers and devotions. | Memento mori--Miscellanea.

Classification: LCC BT825 .N63 2019 | DDC 236/.1--dc23

LC record available at https://lccn.loc.gov/2018036691

Unless otherwise noted, the Scripture quotations contained herein are from the *New Revised Standard Version Bible: Catholic Edition,* copyright © 1989, 1993, Division of Christian Education of the National Council of the Churches of Christ in the United States of America. Used by permission. All rights reserved.

Other Scripture texts in this work are taken from the *New American Bible, Revised Edition* © 2010, 1991, 1986, 1970 Confraternity of Christian Doctrine, Washington, D.C. and are used by permission of the copyright owner. All Rights Reserved. No part of the *New American Bible* may be reproduced in any form without permission in writing from the copyright owner.

Excerpts from Pope Francis' magisterium texts copyright © Libreria Editrice Vaticana. All rights reserved. Used with permission.

Cover art and design by Danielle Victoria Lussier, FSP

Published by Pauline Books & Media, 50 Saint Pauls Avenue, Boston, MA 02130-3491. www.pauline.org

Printed in the U.S.A.

Pauline Books & Media is the publishing house of the Daughters of St. Paul, an international congregation of women religious serving the Church with the communications media.

3 4 5 6 7 8 9   23 22 21 20 19

Contents

Remember Your Death — Change Your Life

YOU ARE GOING TO DIE.

The moment you are born you begin dying. You may die in fifty years, ten years, perhaps tomorrow—or even today. But whenever it happens, death awaits every person, whether rich or poor, young or old, believer or nonbeliever. In *City of God*, Saint Augustine described the startling reality of death as "the very violence with which body and soul are wrenched asunder." A terrifying prospect. So, it's no wonder most people try to ignore their impending death or assume it is far in the future. However, ignoring death will not make it go away. And it may even increase anxiety—because the fearsome truth is that death could come suddenly and forcefully for anyone at any time. Only God knows when each person will die, so preparation for death is an essential spiritual practice, regardless of age.

Memento mori or "remember your death" is a phrase that has been long associated with the practice of remembering the unpredictable and inevitable end of one's life. The spiritual practice of *memento mori* and the symbols and sayings associated with it were particularly popular in the medieval Church. But the tradition of remembering one's death stretches back to the very beginning of salvation history. After the first sin, God reminds Adam and Eve of their mortality: "You are dust, / and to dust you shall return" (Gen 3:19). God's words continue to echo throughout the Hebrew Scriptures, reminding readers of life's brevity, while exhorting them to remember their death. The Book of Sirach urges, "In whatever you do, remember your last days, / and you will never sin." (7:36). The psalmist prays, "Teach us to count our days aright, / that we may gain wisdom of heart" (Ps 90:12). In the New Testament, Jesus exhorts his disciples to pick up their crosses daily and to remember their death as they follow him to the Place of the Skull: "If anyone wishes to come after me, he must deny himself and take up his cross daily and follow me" (Lk 9:23).

Remembering one's death is a practice that philosophers and spiritual teachers, both inside and outside of the Christian tradition, have encouraged for centuries. While the practice certainly can improve the quality of one's earthly life by providing focus and motivation to live well, it could never overcome death itself. Death—whether the natural death of the body or the death of the soul through sin—has always been humanity's most intimidating enemy and its most impossible adversary. Only the Creator of the Universe—the One who first brought everything into existence and continues to maintain all living beings in existence—could overcome death. In the mystery of the incarnation, the Son of God humbled himself and took on human flesh in order to defeat death through his own death. Jesus has defeated humanity's greatest foe—permanent death in sin. All that remains for us to endure is bodily death. And Jesus has transformed even this fearsome reality into the doorway to heaven.

The Cross changes everything. With the triumph of the Cross, remembering one's death involves not only remembering one's mortality but also remembering Christ's victory over death: "Where, O death, is your victory? / Where, O death, is your sting?" (1 Cor 15:55). If we belong to the Lord, we need not fear bodily death. Through his passion, death, and resurrection, Jesus has made salvation available to those who choose to enter into Christ's death, to be buried with him, and to rise with him to new life. Baptism banishes original sin and fills the soul with sanctifying grace—God's own life— that can be renewed and invigorated through the Sacrament of Reconciliation. At Mass, we consume the Eucharist, the Body of Christ. This Body is not the body of a corpse but, rather, the living, risen Body of our Savior who has vanquished death. The Eucharist is heavenly manna, and Jesus promised that it would lead us to heaven: "I am the living bread that came down from heaven; whoever eats this bread will live forever" (Jn 6:51).

Even if one does not believe the Christian message of salvation, the rich, ancient tradition of remembering death can bring joy, focus, and fruitfulness to anyone's life. However, for the Christian, it is a practice that extends beyond the reality of earthly life and bodily death. In the power of Jesus Christ, the Christian practice of *memento mori* reaches past the horizon of this life and into the eternal happiness of heaven. The power of the Cross amplifies the benefits of *memento mori* because the practice is fueled not merely by personal discipline but by God's abundant, living grace. As Christians, we remember our death in order to remember our Life: Jesus Christ. We remember our death in order that our lives may be filled with the Life of Christ, both now and when we enter into the joy of eternal life.

Remembering one's death is an absolutely essential aspect of the Christian life not only because it helps us to live well but also because it helps us to remember what Christ has done for us. Jesus trampled death! *Memento mori* is not a momentary trend but an ancient practice encouraged by Scripture, Jesus, the Church Fathers, and many of the saints. With the grace of God, *memento mori* has the power to change your habits and lead you to holiness. I hope you embrace this ancient and revered practice and make it your own. And always bear in mind: the practice of *memento mori* is more about living than it is about dying.

As you use this devotional, you will be in my prayers.

Remember your death,

 *Theresa Aletheia Noble, FSP*

Live Memento Mori

REMEMBERING YOUR DEATH IS a deeply personal practice that can bring complex emotions to the surface. For this reason, it is important to thoughtfully integrate *memento mori* into your spiritual life. To aid you in this journey, this devotional has daily prompts for reflection activities and journaling. *Remember Your Death: Memento Mori Journal* is an available companion resource that you can use to respond to these prompts. The journal includes inspiring, original *memento mori* quotes as well as quotes from Scripture, Church Fathers, and the saints. The companion journal also contains a section of prayers related to *memento mori*. Whether you use the companion journal or not, it would be helpful to respond to the daily prompts in order to truly welcome the practice of *memento mori* into both your head and heart.

As you integrate *memento mori* into your life, you will find more fruit in the practice if you are also able to connect with those in the community of the Church who are on the same journey. Talk with family and close friends.

Share some of your reflections and reactions with the wider online community with the hashtags #memento-mori and #livemementomori. Death is the fate of every human being, but as Christians we also share the same hope of eternal life. Together on life's journey, we can help one another both to keep our death in mind and our eyes on Jesus.

The Memento Mori Daily Examen

At least once daily, cast your mind ahead to the moment of death so that you can consider the events of each day in this light.

—Saint Josemaría Escrivá

IN HIS RULE, SAINT BENEDICT urged his monks to "keep death daily before your eyes." Benedict urged the remembrance of death so that his monks would live better in this life and keep their eyes on Jesus. Benedict also knew that the practice of remembering death is most effective when observed daily. This Lenten devotional will help you to begin the practice of remembering death daily, if you don't already. But Lent will eventually end, and then you will have to find another way to remember death every day. For this reason, each meditation in this devotional includes an *examen*, a time-honored practice that can be used to incorporate *memento mori* into your daily life.

For those new to it, the *examen* is a review of the day in light of God's love and mercy. Saint Ignatius of Loyola promoted the use of the *examen* to offer God praise and gratitude, identify areas of weakness in which God's help is needed, and to ask for grace for the future. This valuable spiritual practice has been encouraged in the Church for centuries because it has many benefits. The *examen* is a perfect way to incorporate *memento mori* into daily life since making an examen already implicitly evaluates the day in view of heaven. However, the version of the *examen* found below *explicitly* incorporates *memento mori* as a step in which you review the day in the context of your final hours.

How to Make the *Memento Mori* Daily Examen

Step One: Become Aware of God's Presence

Close your eyes and become present to God dwelling within you through your Baptism. Imagine yourself as a child under God's omniscient, compassionate gaze. Try to visualize yourself stepping out your self-centeredness in order to see reality through the loving eyes of God. This step is a crucial beginning to the *examen* as God's perspective on our lives is the only important one.

Step Two: Ask for the Holy Spirit's Guidance

Offer a short prayer asking the Holy Spirit to help you to see the day in the light of God's grace.

Step Three: Review the Day

Ask the questions: "How has God loved me today?" and "How have I loved God and my neighbor today?" Sometimes an obvious moment in the day will jump out—positive or negative—and you can sit with it. However, this step is not like the examination of conscience before confession. Focusing on the negative may come more naturally, but try to note both the positive and negative events of the day and bring them before God in sorrow and thanksgiving.

Step Four: Remember Your Death

Consider the day in view of the last moments of your life. Envision your deathbed scene and reflect on whatever arose in the previous step in the context of eternal life. In this step, thank God for everything in the day that prepared you for heaven. Ask God for the graces you need to better prepare for the moment of your death, which remains unknown. Consider the question: "If I were to die tomorrow, what graces would I need from God?"

Step Five: Look Toward Tomorrow

End by looking forward to the next day. In this step, thank God for the gift of another day of life, should it be God's will. Think of the specific events of the following day, especially those for which you need particular graces. Visualize yourself trusting and acting in God's grace as you live both the trying and joyful moments of the next day. This step, if done faithfully, will lead to concrete behavioral and emotional changes in your life.

Note: At first, the *examen* may take about ten minutes, but once you get used to the practice it can be done in less time. Do not get caught up in doing the steps precisely; there are many different ways to do the *examen*. All that matters is that you get into the rhythm and spirit of the practice and see it bearing fruit.

Hopefully, by the end of Lent, remembering your death and making a regular *examen* will have become almost second nature and a powerful way to grow in holiness!

> Let us prepare ourselves for a good death, for eternity. Let us not lose our time in lukewarmness, in negligence, in our habitual infidelities.
>
> —Saint John Vianney

The Lenten Journey Begins

Saint Paul the Hermit, José de Ribera.

Ash Wednesday

READINGS: J₁ 2:12–18 / P₅ 51:3–4, 5–6ᴀʙ, 12–13, 14, 17 / 2 Cᴏʀ 5:20–6:2 / Mᴛ 6:1–6, 16–18

A clean heart create for me, God;
>   renew within me a steadfast spirit.

—Psalm 51:12

MEMENTO MORI ILLUMINES THE entire penitential season of Lent. Ash Wednesday begins the season by immediately focusing our attention on the theme of remembering death. The Cross—the tool of death that became the tool of our salvation—is traced on Mass-goers foreheads in ash. The priest or minister says the words that God spoke to Adam and Eve as they left the Garden of Eden, "Remember, you are dust and to dust you will return" (see Gn 3:19)—in Latin: *Memento, homo quia pulvis es, et in pulverem reverteris*. This sentiment could be shortened to *memento mori* or "Remember your death."

Remember your death. From the very beginning of salvation history, these words ring out as bells toll before a funeral Mass. Humans are but mortals, mere creatures. God is not some being in the universe that comes into existence, but Existence itself. Every person has life only because God *is* Life. Ash Wednesday is a reminder that humanity needs a Savior because we are but dust and ashes. We need a Savior because the only person who could save us from death is the one who gave us life in the first place. Jesus Christ, who is Life itself, was our last and our only hope.

When we remember death, we meditate on the central mystery of our faith: that death has been transformed by Jesus Christ. Not just a vague and general death but our own *personal* death. Jesus' death and resurrection can have a direct impact on every person's life and death if we accept his saving grace. Therefore, *memento mori* is not an abstract idea, it's personal and concrete. Remembering death for the Christian is absolutely inseparable from remembering what Jesus has done for each one of us.

Meditation on death, however, is not easy. The three traditional practices of Lent are fasting, penance, and almsgiving. And the practice of *memento mori* is definitely a penance. Remembering death is a form of self-denial that leads to conversion. Nonetheless in today's readings—and in fact throughout Scripture—we are encouraged to embrace this practice because it leads to the joy experienced by countless saints. Remembering death in order to truly live cleanses our hearts and renews in us a hopeful, steadfast spirit.

Memento mori does not remain in Lent but leads us through Lent to Easter joy.

Examen and Intercessory Prayer

Review your day (see the Memento Mori Daily Examen, p. 8).

Ask the Holy Spirit to come into your heart this Lent as you meditate on your death and the mysteries of the faith. Pray a Hail Mary for this intention.[*]

> Death is not to be mourned over. First, because it is common and due to all. Next, because it frees us from the miseries of this life. And, lastly, because in the likeness of sleep we are at rest from the toils of this world . . . What grief is there that the grace of the Resurrection does not console? What sorrow is not excluded by the belief that nothing perishes in death? . . . Death is a gain and life a penalty, so that Paul says: "To me to live is Christ and to die is gain" [Phil 1:21]. What is Christ but the death of the body, the breath of life? And so let us die with him, so that we may live with him. Let there be in us a daily practice and inclination to dying. By this separation from bodily desires . . . our soul will learn to withdraw itself and to be "placed on high" where earthly lusts cannot approach and attach themselves. Our soul takes the likeness of death upon herself so she may not incur the penalty of death.
>
> —Saint Ambrose, *On the Death of Satyrus*

---

[*] During the intercessory prayer portion of each meditation, feel free to pray a decade of or the entire Rosary instead of one Hail Mary if you have time that day.

Journaling and Prayer

Take some time to journal on your goals, hopes, and expectations for this season of Lent.

Draw a cross made of ash or write a prayer asking for God's abundant graces on your Lenten journey.

Thursday after Ash Wednesday

READINGS: Dt 30:15–20 / Ps 1:1–2, 3, 4, 6 / Lk 9:22–25

"If anyone wishes to come after me, he must deny himself and take up his cross daily and follow me. For whoever wishes to save his life will lose it, but whoever loses his life for my sake will save it."

—Luke 9:23–24

MEMENTO MORI IS NOT only a practice of the Church Fathers and the saints; Jesus remembered his death his whole life long. In today's Gospel, Jesus tells us that in order to follow him we need to take up our cross *daily*. What does he mean? Is he just speaking metaphorically, urging us to accept life's suffering? Or is he referring to something more literal? Of course, Jesus is not telling us to drag a wooden cross with us to work, social outings, and around the house. But perhaps he is speaking more literally than we might imagine.

As Jesus made his way to the Place of the Skull with the wood of the Cross bearing down on his strong shoulders, what was on his mind? His future success among the Jewish elite? How much money he had saved from carpentry work? His past popularity with the people? No, Jesus was thinking about his death. Jesus did not just begin carrying his Cross on that fateful day. He began the moment he was laid on the wood of the manger. In his divinity, Jesus always knew that his life would end on the Cross. In this way, his entire life was lived in the spirit of *memento mori*. In imitation of Jesus, we too are called to live in this same spirit: "Be imitators of God, as beloved children" (Eph 5:1).

When Jesus tells us to pick up our cross daily, he urges us to envision ourselves with him on the road to the Place of the Skull. Like Christ, we look ahead to death not just sometimes but daily. However unlike him, we don't possess the power to save ourselves from death. But we follow a Savior who does—Jesus has power over life and death. For this reason, we don't just see death at the end of our journey but also what is beyond it. When Jesus invites us to carry our cross, he invites us to follow his entire journey—to the Cross but also to the resurrection. Daily remembrance of death leads us through the Cross to eternal life. The practice is not so much a meditation on death but on the Conqueror of death. Jesus, the Alpha and the Omega, the First and the Last, will lead us through the corridors of death to new life.

Examen and Intercessory Prayer

Review your day (see the Memento Mori Daily Examen, p. 8).

Everyone is asked to carry their cross daily but people with terminal illnesses, those in war-torn countries, and those with dangerous jobs face the possibility of death every day. Pray a Hail Mary for all who face the horizon of death in a more intense way.

No sooner do we begin to live in this dying body than we begin to move ceaselessly toward death. For the whole course of this life (if life we must call it), tends toward death in its mutability. There is certainly no one who is not nearer to death this year than last year, and tomorrow than today, and today than yesterday, and a short time from now than now. . . . For whatever time we live is deducted from our whole term of life, and what remains daily becomes less and less. Our whole life becomes nothing but a race toward death, in which no one is allowed to stand still for a moment, or to go more slowly. Rather, all are driven forward with an impartial momentum and with equal speed. For the one whose life is short spends a day no more swiftly than one whose life is longer. But while the equal moments are impartially snatched from both, the one has a nearer and the other a more remote goal to reach with their equal speed. It is one thing to make a longer journey, and another to walk more slowly. The one, therefore, who spends longer time on the way to death does not proceed at a more leisurely pace, but goes over more ground. Further, if every person begins to die, that is, is in death, as soon as death has begun to show itself . . . then he begins to die so soon as he begins to live. For what else is going on in all his days, hours, and moments, until this slow-working death is fully consummated? . . . A person, then, is never in life from the moment he dwells in this dying rather than living body.

—Saint Augustine, *City of God*

Journaling and Prayer

Imagine following Jesus for a time to the Place of the Skull. Do you consider running away? If so, to what places, possessions, or attachments do you want to run? Reflect on your resistance to following Jesus.

Draw the Place of the Skull and include symbols of hope and everlasting life. Or write a prayer asking Jesus to help you to overcome your fears and resistance as you follow him.

Friday
after Ash Wednesday

READINGS: IS 58:1–9A / PS 51:3–4, 5–6AB, 18–19 / MT 9:14–15

They seek me day after day,
   and desire to know my ways . . .
You shall call, and the LORD will answer,
   you shall cry for help, and he will say: "Here I am!"

—Isaiah 58:2, 9

THE ANGUISHED CRY OF a humanity that cannot save itself echoes throughout salvation history. And God's response echoes back: "Here I am!" The two cries ring out together. Like children unable to cure our own illness or to rise from a fall without help, humanity seeks help, desperately pleading for mercy. And like a mother who rushes to the bed of a sick child or a father who scoops up his child who falls, God stoops down and saves us (see Ps 113:6). God never ceases to respond to our cries for help even if he seems deaf. God's love is like his nature: firm, unchangeable, and enduring as rock. Similarly, God's salvific will is eternal and immutable. In other words, God does not change his mind. God foresaw humanity's rejection before time began and was always going to save us.

While God's love never changes, we, however, are fickle. We forget our need for God and live as if we do not need a Savior. We might begin a prayer for God's help and then think, "I can do this by myself." Or we might never even consider prayer unless we are really frantic, and then it is more an act of superstitious desperation than faith. The sad truth is that sometimes we believe more in our self-sufficiency than we do in God's goodness. But self-sufficiency is a myth. We are not self-sufficient. We are sinners in need of a Savior. No one else but God can provide us with the grace to conquer our sin and make our way to heaven.

Daily meditation on death helps us to smash the myth of self-sufficiency. Our lives completely and utterly depend on God. We would not exist unless God willed it, and we would not continue to exist were it not for God holding us in existence from moment to moment. Even when we rebel, God still holds us in existence. God's Life is the setting and backdrop against which we always live. Meditation on death helps us to understand that because God creates and holds us in existence, we need God's help in absolutely everything. If we learn to rest in this reality rather than run away from it, then our death will only lead us more deeply into Life.

Examen and Intercessory Prayer

Review your day (see the Memento Mori Daily Examen, p. 8).

Think of the people in your life who are more aware of their inability to be self-sufficient: anyone who is disabled, mentally ill, or in prison. Pray a Hail Mary for their needs.

> Death is hideous. But the life beyond the grave that the mercy of God will give us is very desirable. We must by no means lose confidence. For, though we are sinners, we are still far from being as bad as God is merciful and ready to forgive those who repent, who have a will to amend, and who place their hope in Jesus Christ. Death is no longer ignominious, but glorious, since the Son of God has undergone it. For this reason, the Blessed Virgin and all the saints have considered it an advantage to die, in imitation of the Savior, who allowed himself, of his own free consent, to be nailed to the Cross. For death has become, through Jesus Christ, so sweet and amiable, that the angels would regard themselves happy if they could have the privilege of enduring it.
>
> — Saint Francis de Sales

Journaling and Prayer

In what area of your life is the myth of self-sufficiency most at work?

Illustrate or hand letter the following Scripture quote in your journal: "For human beings this is impossible, but for God all things are possible" (Mt 19:26). Or write a prayer asking the Lord to help you realize that without him nothing is possible.

Saturday after Ash Wednesday

READINGS: Is 58:9B–14 / Ps 86: 1–2, 3–4, 5–6 / Lk 5:27–32

"Those who are healthy do not need a physician, but the sick do. I have not come to call the righteous to repentance but sinners."

—Luke 5:31–32

IN TODAY'S GOSPEL, JESUS informs the scribes and Pharisees that he is the Divine Physician. But like many of the scribes and Pharisees, most of us would rather live without need of a physician. When we first feel a cold or a flu coming on, we may respond in denial thinking, "It's just allergies" or "I must have eaten something strange." We plod ahead hoping that our desperation to avoid illness will be enough to ward it off. We believe that if we just ignore our failing bodies, the illness will go away. The way we sometimes deny obvious illness is similar to the way we attempt to ignore sin. We rationalize our sins thinking, "Oh that was pretty minor. I don't think that was a big deal." We evaluate ourselves against other people and think, "I'm not that bad. I mean, comparatively, I'm a pretty good person."

Meanwhile confessionals remain dusty as we all die of the terminal illness of being a "pretty good person." The scourge of our modern age is the widespread acceptance of the "pretty good person" ideal. First, because the bar for goodness is set extremely low. Serious sins are batted away with the roll of an eye and venial sins are either completely ignored or elevated to primary importance, and second, because to be a "pretty good person" is not the same as striving to live a virtuous life. Valuing virtue has all but disappeared, dismissed as too unrealistic, impossible. Instead, we eagerly embrace mediocrity without realizing how easily a "pretty good person" can fall into wretched evil.

Jesus faced a similar problem. He was surrounded by people who did not think they needed a Savior. The scribes and Pharisees' need to control their own destinies enclosed them in graves of self-righteousness (see Mt 23:27). Meanwhile, the people who followed Jesus unreservedly were those in touch with their neediness. They did not ignore the illness of sin infecting their souls. They knew that sin was killing them and that they needed the Divine Physician's healing power.

Like the scribes and Pharisees, we often do not want to admit or to meditate on our sins. But if we refuse to meditate on sin, or spiritual death, then meditating on our physical death will be of no use. When we ignore our sin, we either live in false piety, mediocrity, or evil. Instead, meditating on spiritual death as well as physical death allows us to face the reality that we are like the lepers, the possessed, the adulterous woman, the crippled, the simple fishermen, and the desperately ill people who knew that they needed Jesus' help and begged him for it. Two choices are set before us: admit sin or ignore reality. We may think the choice is unimportant but it is a matter of life and death. In order to make the right choice, we have to first realize that we are ill—deathly ill.

Examen and Intercessory Prayer

Review your day (see the Memento Mori Daily Examen, p. 8).

Ask the Lord to help you to become more aware of your sinfulness so you can ask for help. Pray a Hail Mary for this intention.

> God's mercy toward us is even more wonderful because Christ died not for the righteous or the holy, but for the unrighteous and wicked. The nature of the Godhead could not sustain the sting of death, but at his birth Christ took from us what he could offer for us. For of old, Christ threatened our death with the power of his death, saying by the mouth of Hosea the prophet, "O death, I will be your death, and I will be your destruction, O hell" [13:14]. For by dying he underwent the laws of hell, but by rising again he broke them, and so destroyed the continuity of death so as to make it

temporal instead of eternal. "For as in Adam all die, even so in Christ shall all be made alive" [1 Cor 15:22].

And so, dearly beloved, let what Saint Paul said come to pass, that "they that live, should from now on not live for themselves but for him who died for all and rose again" [2 Cor 5:15]. And because the old things have passed away and all things have become new, let none remain in the old carnal life, but let us all be renewed by daily progress and growth in piety. For however much a person is justified, as long as one remains in this life, one can always be more approved and better. For the one that is not advancing is going back, and the one that is gaining nothing is losing something. Let us run, then, with the steps of faith, by the works of mercy, in the love of righteousness, that keeping the day of our redemption spiritually, not in the old leaven of malice and wickedness, but in the unleavened bread of sincerity and truth [see 1 Cor 5:8], we may deserve to be partakers of Christ's resurrection.

—Saint Leo the Great, *Sermon 59*

Journaling and Prayer

Reflect on a time when you became acutely aware of your sinfulness (in a way that was humbling, helpful, and soul-nourishing, not scrupulous and violent). Thank God for this grace and ask that you may always live in this truth.

Write a letter to the Divine Physician listing all of your most serious sins. Ask the Lord to fill you with the medicine of his grace and love and consider going to confession soon.

First Week of Lent

Saint Jerome in Meditation, Caravaggio.

Sunday

Readings, Year A: Gn 2:7–9; 3:1–7 / Ps 51:3–4, 5–6, 12–13, 17 /
    Rom 5:12–19 / Mt 4:1–11

Year B: Gn 9:8–15 / Ps 25:4–5, 6–7, 8–9 / 1 Pt 3:18–22 /
    Mk 1:12–15

Year C: Dt 26:4–10 / Ps 91:1–2, 10–11, 12–13, 14–15 /
    Rom 10:8–13 / Lk 4:1–13

> Filled with the holy Spirit, Jesus returned from the Jordan and was led by the Spirit into the desert for forty days, to be tempted by the devil.
>
> —Luke 4:1

IN TODAY'S GOSPEL, JESUS enters the desert. There, he is tempted but not intimidated by the devil. Jesus' spirit-filled, divine authority empowers his every response to Satan. Jesus Life battles death. At the end of their duel the devil, death's closest ally, slinks away, angry, baffled, and defeated. On one level, this scenario demonstrates the singular and overwhelming power of the Son of

God. But Jesus also tells us in the Gospel of John, "Whoever believes in me will do the works that I do, and will do greater ones than these" (14:12). For all Christians who seek life and battle death, Jesus' life is a model and an inspiration.

But how exactly can we battle death? Luke notes that Jesus entered the desert "filled with the holy Spirit" (4:1). To describe Jesus as "filled" with the Spirit, Luke uses the Greek word plērēs that appears several more times in the Book of Acts. Stephen, one of the first deacons, is "filled with faith and the Holy Spirit" and with "grace and power" (6:5, 8). Later, when Stephen is martyred, he is also described as "filled with the Holy Spirit" (7:55). Tabitha, a prominent Christian woman in the city of Joppa, is also described by Luke as full of "good deeds and almsgiving" (9:36). The Apostle Barnabas is "filled with the holy Spirit and faith" (11:24). Why is it relevant that Luke uses the same phrase to describe both Jesus and his disciples? Because after Pentecost, Jesus filled his followers with his life. He gave them his own power and authority to combat evil and death, the same power he had used against the devil in the desert.

When we remember our death, we are called to remember also the life-giving power of Baptism that flows from the power of the Cross. In Baptism, we were buried in Christ's death so that we may rise to new life. We enter into spiritual battle armed with this new life, the indwelling of the Holy Spirit. This same Spirit empowers us with divine authority every time we tell Satan to crawl back into his wretched corner of hell. The overflowing, abundant life of baptismal grace enables us, like Tabitha, to be full of good deeds and almsgiving and, like Barnabas and Stephen, to be filled with the power of the Holy Spirit. All the forces of evil and death in our lives and in this world cannot prevail against the saving Life of the Holy Spirit.

Examen and Intercessory Prayer

Review your day (see the Memento Mori Daily Examen, p. 8).

Think of an unbaptized person you know. Pray a Hail Mary that all unbaptized persons might consider receiving the graces of Baptism.

Who is he who has done this? Who is he who has united in peace those who once hated one another? Who else but the beloved Son of the Father, the common Savior of all, Jesus Christ, who by his love underwent all things for our salvation? For even from of old the peace he was to usher in was prophesied, where the Scripture says: "They shall beat their swords into plowshares, and their spears into sickles, and nation shall not take the sword against nation, neither shall they learn war anymore" [Is 2:4]. . . . Even now those [who] cannot endure a single hour without weapons, when they hear Christ's teachings, straightway turn to farming instead of fighting. And instead of arming themselves with weapons they raise them in prayer.

In a word, in place of fighting among themselves, from now on they arm themselves against the devil and against evil spirits, subduing them by self-restraint and virtue of soul. Now this is a proof of the Savior's divinity, since those who could not learn among idols have learned from Jesus and no small exposure to the weakness and nothingness of demons and idols. For demons, knowing their own weakness, tried to set people at war against one another, in fear that they should cease from mutual strife and turn to battle against demons. Those who become disciples of Christ, instead of warring with each other, stand arrayed against demons by their habits and their virtuous actions. And they rout them and mock their captain, the devil. In youth these disciples are self-restrained, in temptations they endure, in labors they persevere, when insulted they are patient, when robbed they make light of it: and, wonderful as it is, they despise even death and become martyrs for Christ.

—Saint Athanasius, *On the Incarnation of the Word*

Journaling and Prayer

What is your desert right now? Is it a particular situation? A difficult person? Do you feel spiritually attacked? Bring your troubles to Jesus and then listen to his response.

Write a prayer, asking the Holy Spirit to help you to tap into the power within you through Baptism.

Monday

READINGS: Lv 19:1–2, 11–18 / Ps 19:8, 9, 10, 15 / Mt 25:31–46

"Then the king will say to those on his right, 'Come, you who are blessed by my Father. Inherit the kingdom prepared for you from the foundation of the world. For I was hungry and you gave me food, I was thirsty and you gave me drink, a stranger and you welcomed me, naked and you clothed me, ill and you cared for me, in prison and you visited me.' Then the righteous will answer him and say, 'Lord, when did we see you hungry and feed you, or thirsty and give you drink? When did we see you a stranger and welcome you, or naked and clothe you? When did we see you ill or in prison, and visit you?' And the king will say to them in reply, 'Amen, I say to you, whatever you did for one of these least brothers of mine, you did for me.'"

—Matthew 25:34–40

JESUS CHRIST HAS MADE DEATH the doorway to eternal life. So, when we stop to meditate on death, we also are simultaneously meditating on eternal life. In today's Gospel, Jesus tells us how we should live in order to reach eternal life. With very clear and frank language, he stresses that only friends of the poor and the defenseless will enter the kingdom of heaven. He does not select just one group of vulnerable persons, but lists group after group: the hungry, the thirsty, strangers, the naked, the ill, and prisoners. The variety in Jesus' list suggests that it is not meant to be restrictive. We could add the unborn, the elderly, workers, refugees, and the list goes on. While Jesus is normally quite concise, he twice repeats the list of people we are called to help, those who are Christ on earth. The repetition signals the importance that God places on serving the poor and vulnerable.

Dorothy Day once wrote in *The Catholic Worker*: "I firmly believe that our salvation depends on the poor." Service to the poor is not ancillary to the Christian life. This service or lack thereof can either lead us to eternal life or to permanent death. God's children are called to have hearts of compassion for every person in need and to acknowledge the countless cries of sorrow and terrified faces of desperation in our world. Of course, some of us may feel called to work with a specific group. Nevertheless, Jesus is clear that a Christian's generosity of heart should never be limited. We are called to open our hearts to the diverse and sometimes conflicting needs and cries of humanity. Jesus tells us that this call is not a bonus, but is central to the Christian life and leads to eternal life.

Some Christians may downplay serving the poor and vulnerable as if it were an optional hobby that only some are called to take up. But Jesus is quite candid: those who do not do works of mercy will be sent "into the eternal fire prepared for the devil and his angels" (Mt 25:41). Saint John Chrysostom, commenting on this Gospel, wrote with similar bluntness and emphasis, "There is no pardon, no, none for him who does not do works of mercy." This Gospel should disturb us. It should also motivate us to find life in serving Christ in the poor. The road to heaven is paved with works of mercy, and these works are just as much for our well-being as they are for others. In serving the poor, we find Christ our Life. In serving the vulnerable, we evade death and find true and lasting life.

Examen and Intercessory Prayer

Review your day (see the Memento Mori Daily Examen, p. 8).

Reflect for a moment on a group of vulnerable persons close to your heart. Now, think of another group of vulnerable persons whose needs you find more difficult to care about. Pray a Hail Mary for both groups.

> "Watch therefore, for you know not the day or the hour" [Mt 25:13]. Do you see how [Jesus] continually adds this, showing how awful our ignorance is concerning our departure? Where are those people now who throughout their life were remiss [in helping the poor] but when criticized said, "At the time of my death, I shall leave money to the poor." Let them listen to these words and make amends. For indeed many have failed

to do this at their death, having been snatched away at once. . . . Knowing these things, let us contribute wealth, diligence, protection, and all things for our neighbor's advantage. . . . For you are not poorer than that widow [see Lk 21:1–4]; you are not less instructed than Peter and John, who were both unlearned and ignorant men [see Acts 4:13]. But nevertheless, they showed forth zeal, did all things for the common good, and reached heaven. Nothing is as pleasing to God as to live for the common good. For this end, God gave us speech, hands, feet, strength of body and mind, and understanding, that we might use all these things, both for our own salvation and for our neighbor's advantage.

—Saint John Chrysostom, *Homily 78 on Matthew*

Journaling and Prayer

Everyone is called to help their neighbors, but God often has a special call or focus for each person. What is yours? Take some time to pray and reflect on your unique call to help those in need.

Sketch a vulnerable person from the group that you feel called to serve. Or write a prayer asking the Lord to help you discern how you can provide for the needs of the poor.

Tuesday

READINGS: Is 55:10–11 / Ps 34:4–5, 6–7, 16–17, 18–19 / Mt 6:7–15

Just as from the heavens
    the rain and snow come down
And do not return there
    till they have watered the earth,
    making it fertile and fruitful . . .
So shall my word be
    that goes forth from my mouth;
It shall not return to me empty,
    but shall do what pleases me,
    achieving the end for which I sent it.

—Isaiah 55:10–11

IN TODAY'S READINGS, THE Prophet Isaiah describes a word that goes forth from the mouth of God like rain watering the earth. From the beginning, God watered the world, desiring that all within it be fruitful and full of life. But in our sin, we turned away from this life-giving water and embraced death. In our prideful need to control, we ran from the rain of the Word to the desert oasis of death. Regardless of what we do, however, God continues to pour his saving Word like rain upon the earth. God's goodness does not change despite how we might behave: "He makes his sun rise on the bad and the good, and causes rain to fall on the just and the unjust" (Mt 5:45).

Jesus describes himself as "Living Water" (see Jn 4:10). He is the culmination of Isaiah's prophecy and God's salvific action in the world, who comes "to us like the rain, like spring rain that waters the earth" (Hos 6:3). When the soldier pierced Jesus' side while he was hanging on the Cross, blood and water (see Jn 19:34) poured out like rain. Some have speculated that both blood and water gushed forth from Jesus' side because the soldier's lance punctured Jesus' heart. The Word of God, not satisfied with merely speaking his word of love, showered the earth with blood and water from his Sacred Heart. Christ's heart-blood poured itself into our sinful hearts, bringing fruitfulness from dry ground.

Christian meditation on death is most profitable when we make efforts to continually accept the rain of God's grace that pours itself into our hearts through the sacraments. Saint John Chrysostom observed that the blood and water that gushed from Jesus Christ's dying body are symbols of the gift of the sacraments to the Church. How could we ignore these intimate gifts in our lives? Baptism, the Eucharist, the sacrament of Reconciliation, and Anointing of the Sick particularly help our souls, dry and desiccated by sin, to become vibrant once again. The early Church Father Tertullian once compared Christians to "little fishes" because we are born in the waters of Baptism. When we feel like we are plodding through the sands of the desert instead of swimming in the waters of God's grace, we can always ask the Holy Spirit to well up in our hearts. God never tires of our return. Time and again the waters of God's grace wash over our stony, deadened hearts, turning them to living hearts of flesh (see Ez 36:26). The steady rain of God's grace in our hearts helps us to live well on this earth and will lead us "to springs of life-giving water" (Rev 7:17) in heaven.

Examen and Intercessory Prayer

Review your day (see the Memento Mori Daily Examen, p. 8).

Bring to mind any RCIA candidates you may know. Pray a Hail Mary for all of the RCIA candidates in the Church who are preparing for the sacraments.

> The Spirit descended upon the Son of God, made the Son of man, and became accustomed in fellowship with him to dwell in the human race, to rest with human beings, and to dwell in the workmanship of God, working the will of the Father in them, and renewing them from their old habits into the newness of Christ. David once asked for this Spirit for the human race, saying, "And establish me with your all-governing Spirit" [see Ps 51:12]. The Spirit also, as Luke says, descended at the day of Pentecost upon the disciples after the Lord's ascension, having power to admit all nations to the entrance of life, and to the opening of the new

covenant. From then on, the Spirit brought distant tribes to unity, and with one accord in all languages they uttered praise to God and offered the Father the first fruits of all nations. . . .

As a compacted lump of dough cannot be formed of dry wheat without liquid and neither can a loaf possess unity, so, in like manner, neither could we, being many, be made one in Christ Jesus without the water from heaven. And as dry earth does not yield [fruit] unless it receives moisture, in like manner we also, being originally a dry tree, could never have brought fruit to life without the voluntary rain from above. For our bodies have received unity among themselves by means of that laver that leads to incorruption; but our souls [have received unity] by means of the Spirit.

—Saint Irenaeus, *Against Heresies*

Journaling and Prayer

Pope Francis often calls the Holy Spirit the "forgotten one" because we can easily lose sight of the Spirit's power in our lives. Reflect on how much you call upon the Holy Spirit in your life and whether you could call upon the Holy Spirit more.

Write a prayer asking the Holy Spirit to flood your heart and your life.

Wednesday

READINGS: JON 3:1–10 / PS 51:3–4, 12–13, 18–19 / LK 11:29–32

> "This generation is an evil generation; it seeks a sign, but no sign will be given it, except the sign of Jonah."
>
> —Luke 11:29

SOME FOLLOWERS OF JESUS were hungry for sign after miraculous sign. Their focus was not on Jesus' divine identity but on what he could do for them. In today's Gospel, Jesus tells the people that the only sign they will receive is the sign of Jonah. Of course, at this point Jesus has performed many signs and wonders: healings, exorcisms, feeding thousands of people with just a handful of loaves, and raising the dead. Jesus is a God-man of signs and wonders. And yet, some people still did not believe. So, Jesus tells them that they will have one final sign.

In the Gospel of Matthew, Jesus is more specific about the nature of this sign, "Just as Jonah was in the belly of the whale three days and three nights, so will the Son of Man be in the heart of the earth three days and three nights" (Mt 12:40). Explaining this cryptic verse, Augustine wrote: "As Jonah passed from the ship to the belly of the whale, so Christ passed from the Cross to the sepulcher, or into the abyss of death." The sign of Jonah, therefore, is the three days Jesus spent in the tomb and his final descent on Holy Saturday into the "abyss of death."

Death is the deepest, darkest descent into human reality that God could have taken upon himself. Jesus' entire life was immersed in this dynamic of descent. As Saint Paul writes, Christ "emptied" himself and "humbled himself, becoming obedient to death, even death on a cross" (Phil 2:7–8). The sign of all signs is the Son of God's descent from heaven even unto death, and his subsequent ascent in the resurrection and the ascension. If the people were to see these events unfold and still not believe, then nothing else would ever convince them. All the healings and miracles in the world would not persuade anyone who remains unmoved in the face of the astounding descent and ascent of God—a God who loves humanity so much that he joins us in death.

The dynamic of descent to ascent that Christ modeled for us is the same dynamic that we follow in the Christian life. We are called to make our own the words of John the Baptist when Jesus' ministry began: "He must increase; I must decrease" (Jn 3:30). As we descend in humility, we descend into the death of

Jesus. This descent on our journey to heaven is unavoidable. Jesus' life is our roadmap. There is no other way to heaven. In order to rise, we must follow Christ to his death. We are called to embrace humility and to die to ourselves in order that Christ may live in us (see Gal 2:20). We can either accept the Sign of Jonah in our own lives or reject life itself—descent and death is the only way to life.

Examen and Intercessory Prayer

Review your day (see the Memento Mori Daily Examen, p. 8).

Think of the Catholics you know and love who no longer attend Mass. Pray a Hail Mary that all Catholics will frequent the sacraments.

> The bodily Nativity of the Son of God took nothing from and added nothing to his Majesty, because his unchangeable substance could neither be diminished nor increased. For "the Word became flesh" does not signify that the nature of God was changed into flesh, but that the Word took the flesh into the unity of his Person. . . . We could not be released from the chains of eternal death in any other way but by him becoming humble in our nature, who remained Almighty in his own. . . . What mind can grasp this mystery, what tongue can express this gracious act? Sinfulness returns to guiltlessness and the old nature becomes new; strangers receive adoption and outsiders enter upon an inheritance. The ungodly begin to be righteous, the miserly benevolent, the incontinent chaste, the earthly heavenly. And where does this change

come from, save by the right hand of the Most High? For the Son of God came to destroy the works of the devil [see 1 Jn 3:8], and has so united himself with us and us with him that the descent of God to our estate became our own exaltation to God's.

—Saint Leo the Great, *Sermon 27*

Journaling and Prayer

Do you live as one who believes in the Sign of Jonah? How does your belief in Jesus' resurrection change your life?

Draw an image of the connection between Jonah and Jesus, or handletter Saint Augustine's quote (p. 44).

Thursday

READINGS: EST C:12, 14–16, 23–25 / PS 138:1–2AB, 2CDE–3, 7C–8 / MT 7:7–12

Then [Esther] prayed to the LORD, the God of Israel, saying: "My LORD, you alone are our King. . . . Put in my mouth persuasive words in the presence of the lion [the king], and turn his heart to hatred for our enemy, so that he and his co-conspirators may perish. Save us by your power, and help me, who am alone and have no one but you, LORD.

—Esther C:14–15, 24–25

ESTHER WAS A MEMBER of a persecuted minority in a land full of danger. But God's plan for her did not involve hiding and cowering in fear. Rather, God asked Esther to undertake the terrifying risk of reaching out to the very people who endangered her life. Only in the power of God could she hope to succeed. As believers, we too often find ourselves in similar situations. The world can be like a foreign land with the potential to bring death to both our bodies and souls. But like Esther, God asks us to trust in his power and to courageously risk physical death if necessary. We can do so without fear because we know that sin—not physical death—is the greatest danger in this world.

Like Esther, we live amid death's co-conspirators who aid and abet the spread of evil in their own souls and in the souls of others. Saint Paul described these people as those who "conduct themselves as enemies of the cross of Christ" (Phil 3:18). Some spread death knowingly, others out of desperate ignorance, and still others out of a desire for power, love, or to satisfy the ego. Unfortunately, we cannot draw a stark dividing line between ourselves and death's co-conspirators. All of us make ourselves enemies of the saving Cross of Christ when we sin. We all, at some point, have conspired with evil. Yet, even when we serve for a time in the courts of the evil one, our King always welcomes back those with repentant hearts.

Meditation on death includes meditation on the King of Life in whose court we strive to serve. As we contemplate death, our King of Life will call us away from the courts of this world to serve in his court, the kingdom of heaven on earth. Each time we choose virtue instead of sin, life instead of death, we sing God's praises in the court of our heavenly King. Our King, Jesus Christ, has tread upon death and saved us from sin! Our King defeated evil from the throne of the Cross. Our King turns us—co-conspirators of evil and death—into friends of God. Therefore, even when we stand before the lions of this world and amidst the co-conspirators of death, we have nothing to fear.

Examen and Intercessory Prayer

Review your day (see the Memento Mori Daily Examen, p. 8).

Consider all of the Christians and religious minorities in the world who suffer for their faith. Pray a Hail Mary for their consolation and protection.

I saw in a vision Pomponius the deacon come to the door of the prison and knock hard upon it. . . . He said to me: "Perpetua, we await you. Come." And he took my hand, and we began to go through rugged and winding places. At last, breathing heavily, we arrived at the amphitheatre, and he led me into the middle of the arena. He said to me: "Be not afraid; I am here with you and labor together with you." And he went away. I saw many people watching closely. Because I knew I was condemned, I marveled that beasts were not sent out against me.

A certain Egyptian, horrible in appearance, came out with his helpers to fight against me. . . . There came forth a man of such great stature that he rose higher than the very top of the amphitheater. He wore a loose tunic and a purple robe between two bands over the middle of the breast; with shoes curiously wrought in gold and silver. He carried a rod like a master of gladiators and a green branch with golden apples. And he called for silence and said: "If the Egyptian conquers this woman, he will slay her with the sword. And if she conquers him, she will receive this branch." And he went away. [The Egyptian and I] drew near to one another and began to buffet one another. He tried to trip up my feet, but I struck his face with my heels. And I was lifted up into the air and began to thrust at him. . . . I joined my hands so as to twine my fingers with one another and I took hold of his head, and he fell upon his face; and I trod upon his head. The people began to shout, and my helpers began to exult. I went to the master of gladiators and received the branch. He kissed me and said, "Daughter, peace be with you." And I began to go with glory to the gate called the Gate of Life. And I awoke; and I understood that I should fight, not with beasts but against the devil, and I knew that the victory was mine.

—Saint Perpetua's Third Vision, *The Passion of the Holy Martyrs Perpetua and Felicity*

Journaling and Prayer

Think of a time that you felt like you were standing before the lions of this world. Did you trust in God? How did you handle the situation? How could you have handled it better with God's grace?

Write a prayer of thanksgiving to God for the times he has helped you to courageously speak for his kingdom of life and to spread God's love to those around you.

Friday

Readings: Ez 18:21–28 / Ps 130:1–4, 5–8 / Mt 5:20–26

"I tell you, unless your righteousness surpasses that of the scribes and Pharisees, you will not enter into the kingdom of heaven."

—Matthew 5:20

THE PHARISEES AND SCRIBES of Jesus' day are often caricatured as self-righteous men so lost in their pride that they missed the long-awaited Messiah standing right before them. Even the word "Pharisee" now commonly refers to a sanctimonious, hypocritical religious person. But Jesus' relationship with the Pharisees was far more complex. The Pharisees commendably dedicated their whole lives to God and sought holiness and virtue in the law. Jesus recognized this and reached out to them, knowing and desiring the conversion that he knew was possible.

In today's Gospel, though Jesus may appear to insult the Pharisees, he is actually praising them by holding up their way of life as the highest bar of righteousness. But Jesus also points to something new that is happening. A way of life that would have otherwise been impossible is now possible: to surpass the righteousness of the Pharisees. Humans are not naturally capable of virtue surpassing the Pharisee's adherence to the law, which was quite rigorous. But the grace of Jesus Christ that gives salvation also gives the supernatural power to live a way of life previously thought to be impossible.

We can approach meditation on death as just one way to strive to grow in virtue through self-discipline. And this is admirable—holiness does require self-discipline. But the best we can do through only our own strength is not enough to save us. Regular, disciplined meditation on death, though good and useful, can never save us from death itself. Only the unearned, precious, salvific, and sanctifying grace of Jesus Christ can save. Christ's grace changes the way we remember our death. As Christians, when we contemplate our death, we enter *into* the death of Jesus Christ. We remember death not from our own perspective but from Christ's perspective. We remember that death has been conquered. This way of meditating on death is far more powerful than a secular remembrance of death, which is focused merely on physical death and self-discipline. *Memento mori* from Christ's perspective fundamentally and powerfully changes lives.

Examen and Intercessory Prayer

Review your day (see the Memento Mori Daily Examen, p. 8).

Think of a few people in your life who are kind, caring, and generous, but who do not go to church. Pray a Hail Mary that they may find even more life and virtue in the sacraments.

> In the race of the spiritual life all the virtues run, but only perseverance "receives the prize" [see 1 Cor 9:24]. It is not the beginner in virtue but "he who perseveres until the end who shall be saved" [see Mt 24:13]. Saint John Chrysostom asks, "What is the use of seeds sprouting if afterward they wither and die?" None whatsoever! . . . Persevere in your virtuous habits. Make it a practice always and constantly to increase in the performance of good works. Wage the war of Christ with all your might. Practice and increase in virtue up to the very moment of death. Then, when your last moment comes and your life is brought to a close, God will give you the crown of honor and glory as the prize and reward of your labor. Your most beloved Lord Jesus Christ has assured you of this. These are his words, written for your instruction by the inspired writer . . . "Be faithful unto death, and I will give you the crown of life" [see Rev 2:10]. What is this crown if not the reward of eternal life? The heart of every Christian ought to burn with the desire of winning this reward. In value there is nothing comparable to it, it is priceless.
>
> —Saint Bonaventure, *Holiness of Life*

Journaling and Prayer

Reflect on one way you have been failing in virtue. Do you rely on your own power to overcome sin? Have you turned to the sacraments and trusted in God's grace? Take some time to talk about this with God.

Write a prayer asking God to help you to overcome a vice that seems impossible to conquer.

Saturday

READING: DT 26:16–19 / PS 119:1–2, 4–5, 7–8 / MT 5:43–48

"So be perfect, just as your heavenly Father is perfect."

—Matthew 5:48

IN TODAY'S GOSPEL, JESUS URGES the people to "be perfect." This phrase can have many different connotations. One might think that Jesus is urging people to repress painful emotions, paste smiles on their faces, and pretend that everything is rosy. However, as Christians, we are not called to be inauthentic, plasticized versions of ourselves. Rather, God's perfection is perfection in love, perfection in holiness. Holiness magnifies our true identity. When we live a life of holiness, we allow God to chip away at our imperfections until the work of art he created begins to shine through.

Holiness is never neat and artificial, it's a messy business. God's way of perfect love is untidy. Perfection is Saint Francis of Assisi kissing a leper. Perfection is Saint Thérèse of Lisieux allowing dirty dishwater to be spattered on her and not getting angry. Perfection is Saint Isaac Jogues demanding to return to New France after he was tortured and his thumb cut off. Perfection is following in the footsteps of Jesus who, dripping blood and sweat and covered in dust, slowly made his way to the Place of the Skull to accept a horrific and torturous death.

Holiness can seem like an overwhelming task, especially when we consider the entire length of our lives. But we could die tomorrow. So, better to approach perfection in love simply, one moment at a time.

"Jesus, help me to be a saint in this conversation."

"Jesus, help me to be a saint as I get my kids ready for bed."

"Jesus, help me to be a saint as I greet that person who was rude to me yesterday."

Jesus' way of perfect love is not easy to imitate, but it's also not as hard as we think. Holiness is only a weighty burden when we mistakenly assume that it's all up to us. It's not. Our perfection in holiness is up to God. We only have to cooperate, and even that is grace. Supported by the grace of our Baptism, instant by instant, while being gentle with ourselves and begging God to aid us—let's be perfect. Let's be saints and let's begin now. Because, who knows, we might die tomorrow.

Examen and Intercessory Prayer

Review your day (see the Memento Mori Daily Examen, p. 8).

Think of some people in your life who are models of God's love. Say a Hail Mary for their intentions.

Death is transformed by Christ. Jesus, the Son of God, also himself suffered the death that is part of the human condition. Yet, despite his anguish as he faced death, he accepted it in an act of complete and free submission to his Father's will. The obedience of Jesus has transformed the curse of death into a blessing. . . .

In death, God calls man to himself. Therefore the Christian can experience a desire for death like Saint Paul's: "My desire is to depart and be with Christ." He can transform his own death into an act of obedience and love toward the Father, after the example of Christ: "My earthly desire has been crucified . . . there is living water in me, water that murmurs and says within me: Come to the Father" (Saint Ignatius of Antioch). "I want to see God and, in order to see him, I must die" (Saint Teresa of Avila). "I am not dying; I am entering life" (Saint Thérèse of Lisieux). The Christian vision of death receives privileged expression in the liturgy of the Church: "Lord, for your faithful people life is changed, not ended. When the body of our earthly dwelling lies in death we gain an everlasting dwelling place in heaven" (Roman Missal).

Death is the end of man's earthly pilgrimage, of the time of grace and mercy which God offers him so as to work out his earthly life in keeping with the divine plan, and to decide his ultimate destiny. When "the single course of our earthly life" is completed, we shall not return to other earthly lives: "It is appointed for men to die once" (Heb 9:27). There is no "reincarnation" after death.

The Church encourages us to prepare ourselves for the hour of our death. In the litany of the saints, for instance, she has us pray: "From a sudden and unforeseen death, deliver us, O Lord" (Roman Missal); to ask the Mother of God to intercede for us "at the hour of our death" in the *Hail Mary;* and to entrust ourselves to Saint Joseph, the patron of a happy death.

—*Catechism of the Catholic Church*,
nos. 1009, 1011–1014

Journaling and Prayer

What kind of person do you hope to be at the point of your death? Reflect on the ways you can live your life now to be true to the kind of person you were made to be.

If you become a canonized saint in the Church (anything is possible!), what would your saint icon look like? Draw or write the symbols that would be included. What would you be holding? (This exercise can help you to get in touch with the core gifts that God is calling you to share.)

Second Week of Lent

Saint Catherine of Siena, Cristofano Allori.

Sunday

READINGS, YEAR A: GEN 12:1–4A / Ps 33:4–5, 18–20, 22 / 2 TIM 1:8B–10 /
MT 17:1–9

YEAR B: GEN 22:1–2, 9A, 10–13, 15–18 / Ps 116:10, 15–19 / ROM 8:31B–34 /
MK 9:2–10

YEAR C: GEN 15:5–12, 17–18 / Ps 27:1, 7–9, 13–14 / PHIL 3:17–4:1 /
LK 9:28B–36

Peter and his companions had been overcome by
sleep, but becoming fully awake, they saw his glory.

—Luke 9:32

AGING. PAIN. ILLNESS. BROKEN relationships. Death. All
humans experience these things at one point or
another. Yet we often try to convince ourselves that we
can somehow avoid them. We irrationally deny reality
and insist on being the exception to the expected.
Unfortunately, when something bad does happen to us,
our unmet expectations compound our suffering. Re-
fusing to accept the unavoidable, we try to escape it.
We might try the hedonistic route, drowning out the

sighs of our sorrows with sighs of pleasure. Or we might avoid suffering by pretending to be stoic and immune to it. Or we might try to control our future, deluding ourselves that we can somehow escape suffering. Unfortunately, none of these options free us from suffering. Instead, they numb our emotions or fill us with anxiety and only intensify our pain in the long run.

Avoidance of suffering is like an anesthesia that puts us into a deep, temporary slumber to help us cope with life by avoiding reality. We can sleep through life, whether by drowning suffering with pleasure or pretending suffering doesn't exist. But when we do these things, we miss both the painful and the wondrous. The disciples slept not only before the terror in the Garden of Gethsemane but also before the wonder of the Transfiguration. To avoid suffering is to avoid the beauty of life. Suffering is part of life on earth. To suffer is to live. When we avoid suffering, we avoid living. And when we try to avoid a part of living, we end up avoiding life entirely. We embrace death before natural death.

Jesus, the Son of God, the only one who could have avoided suffering if he wanted to, chose to die on a Cross. The way beyond sorrow and suffering, therefore, is to follow Jesus through it, not to avoid it. Jesus has shown us the way to life. Our All-powerful God chose to experience the depths of human pain and sorrow and, in this way, transformed it. Knowing this, some of us still think we can somehow supersede the human condition if we just try really hard or read enough self-help books. However, rather than striving to overcome our humanness and frailty, we are better off remembering it. To remember death is a suffering. So, in order to practice *memento mori*, we must first accept suffering. Keeping in mind our vulnerability and mortality can be painful. But it ensures that we cooperate with and are awake to witness the transfiguration that God wants to work in our souls. Remembering death keeps us awake, focused, and ready for whatever might happen—both the excruciatingly difficult and the breathtakingly beautiful.

Examen and Intercessory Prayer

Review your day (see the Memento Mori Daily Examen, p. 8).

Bring to mind someone you know who is addicted to drugs or alcohol. Pray a Hail Mary for healing and recovery for all addicts.

Plato thinks that a wise man's whole life ought to be a meditation on death and philosophers praise the sentiment and extol it to the skies. But much greater in power are the words of the Apostle: "I die daily through your glory" [see 1 Cor 15:31]. For to have an ideal is one thing, to realize it another. It is one thing to live so as to die, another to die so as to live. The sage and Christian must both die: but the one always dies out of his glory, the other into it. . . . Oh! If we could but go up a watchtower so high that from it we might behold the whole earth spread out under our feet. Then I would show you the wreck of the world, nation warring against nation and kingdom in collision with kingdom; some tortured, others put to the sword, others swallowed up by the waves, some dragged away into slavery; here a wedding, there a funeral; some born here, some dying there; some living in affluence, others begging for their bread . . . all the inhabitants of the world alive now but destined soon to pass away. Language is inadequate to a theme so vast, and all that I can say must fall short of the reality.

Let us return then to ourselves, and coming down from the skies let us look for a few moments upon what more closely concerns us. Are you conscious, I would ask, of the stages of your growth? Can you fix the time when you became a baby, a child, a youth, an adult, an old person? Every day we are changing, every day we are dying, and yet we fancy ourselves eternal. The very moments I spend in dictation, in writing, in reading over what I write, and in correcting it, are moments taken from my life. Every dot that my secretary makes is a moment gone from my allotted time. We write letters and reply to those of others, our missives cross the sea, and, as the vessel plows its furrow through wave after wave, the moments we have to live vanish one by one. Our only gain is that we are thus knit together in the love of Christ.

—Saint Jerome, *Letter 60*

Journaling and Prayer

What are some ways that you "sleep" through life? Too much electronics? Streaming TV shows and movies? Shopping? Acquiring money? Working too much? Worrying? Write a list and quietly bring it before God.

Write a prayer asking for the grace to not numb your pain but to grow through it with God.

Monday

Readings: Dn 9:4b–10 / Ps 79:8, 9, 11, 13 / Lk 6:36–38

> Help us, God our savior,
>> on account of the glory of your name.
> Deliver us, pardon our sins
>> for your name's sake.
> Let the groaning of the imprisoned come in before you;
>> in accord with the greatness of your arm
>> preserve those doomed to die.
>
> —Psalm 79:9, 11

SINCE THE BEGINNING OF TIME, humanity has labored under the illusion that freedom is merely the opportunity to choose either good or bad. We want freedom on our terms. We reject the idea that freedom is only found in choosing the good, because that would require us to submit our will to something—or Someone—else. We revel in autonomy because we want to make our own choices and forge our own paths. We refuse to accept subjugation of any kind. However, many of us soon realize the truth revealed in today's readings: that choosing anything other than the good leads not to freedom but to imprisonment. When we don't choose the good, we inevitably are enslaved to the idol of our ego.

Worse than any cement building surrounded by barbed wire, sin imprisons us. No matter what, we are going to serve *something.* God or sin can be our master, and obedience to the divine is far sweeter than obedience to our basest desires. But often we ignore the truth that choosing God leads to true freedom and instead rationalize choosing sin. As we do, sin slowly chokes our reason and wraps like shackles around our minds and hearts. All of humanity groans under these chains of sin. We are not strong enough to smash the chains that bind us. Our God of freedom—whose very nature is goodness and free, unbounded Being itself—is the only one who can free humanity from sin.

When we remember death, we must also bear in mind that God is the one who holds "the keys to death and the netherworld" (Rev 1:18). Jesus Christ's victory over death demolished the sin that enslaved us. Through his death and resurrection, Jesus has shared the freedom of grace and poured it into our hearts. Over and over, we are called to reject the master of sin and to accept Jesus as the gentle Lord of our lives. When we feel imprisoned by bad choices, we can run to Jesus, who unchains us from death and leads us to life.

Examen and Intercessory Prayer

Review your day (see the Memento Mori Daily Examen, p. 8).

Think of someone you know who is in either a literal or a figurative prison. Pray a Hail Mary for all prisoners, especially those on death row.

If anyone here is a slave of sin, let that person promptly prepare through faith for the new birth into freedom and adoption. And having put off the miserable bondage of sin, and taken on the most blessed bondage of the Lord, so may that person be counted worthy to inherit the kingdom of heaven. Put off, by confession, the old self, which waxes corrupt after the lusts of deceit, that you may put on the new self. . . . Now is the season of confession: confess what you have done in word or in deed, by night or by day; confess in an acceptable time, and in the day of salvation [see 2 Cor 6:2] receive the heavenly treasure. . . . Blot out from your mind all earthly care: for you are running for your soul. You are utterly forsaking the things of the world: little are the things which you are forsaking and great what the Lord gives. Forsake things present, and put your trust in things to come. Have you not run so many circles of years busied by the vain things of the world, and have you not forty days to be free [for prayer], for your own soul's sake? Be still, and know that I am God, Scripture says [see Ps 46:10]. Excuse yourself from idle words: neither gossip, nor lend a willing ear to gossipers; but rather be prompt to prayer. Show in ascetic exercise that your heart is courageous. Cleanse your vessel, that you may receive grace more abundantly.

For though remission of sins is given equally to all, the communion of the Holy Spirit is bestowed in proportion to each person's faith. If you have labored little, you receive little; but if you have wrought much, the reward is great. You are running for yourself, see to your own interest. . . . Wrestle for your soul, especially in days such as these.

—Saint Cyril of Jerusalem, *Catechetical Lecture 1*

Journaling and Prayer

Take some time to prepare yourself to go to confession. Examine your conscience. Choose two times when you have sinned recently and ask God to help you see the situation clearly. Conclude this time by asking God to help you to trust in his abundant mercy and make plans to receive the sacrament of Reconciliation.

Draw a picture of the chains of sin around your heart. Or write a prayer asking Jesus to smash the chains of sin that enslave you.

Tuesday

Readings: Is 1:10, 16–20 / Ps 50:8–9, 16bc–17, 21, 23 / Mt 23:1–12

Come now, let us set things right,
    says the Lord:
Though your sins be like scarlet,
    they may become white as snow;
Though they be red like crimson,
    they may become white as wool.
If you are willing, and obey,
    you shall eat the good things of the land;
But if you refuse and resist,
    you shall be eaten by the sword:
    for the mouth of the Lord has spoken!
                 —Isaiah 1:18–20

IN TODAY'S PASSAGE FROM ISAIAH, God almost sounds like an exasperated parent, "Come now, let us set things right" (1:18). Perhaps Isaiah wanted to communicate how desperately God desires to provide us with the graces we need for our souls to become "white as snow." God wants our cooperation in our sanctification. Yet we are often unwilling or unable to do what is right. We need God's help even in willing to do what is good. Cooperation begins with the plea, "Help me to do what I don't want to do! Help me to want to do what I don't want to do!" This plea is all God needs to join our wills to his so that he can cleanse us and lead us to eternal life.

However, if we refuse God's help, Isaiah warns of dire consequences, "You shall be eaten by the sword" (1:20). These words can strike fear in the heart. But we need not fear a sword of our own making. God—All-Powerful Goodness itself—wants to save us. If we are willing, God will smash the swords of death that we fashion with our sin. However, even faced with the startling consequences of sin, we are still sometimes unwilling to give ourselves over to God. We resist what will lead us to life and refuse God's help in making things right. Thankfully, God will continue to cajole and urge us to accept life until our dying breath.

A constant battle rages within each person until death. Will we enthrone our ego, or the King of heaven? The moment we push our ego off the throne and enthrone Jesus, our ego battles with the help of the devil to depose God once again. Yet, we have no reason to fear this constant battle—a sign of our tendency toward sin—if we are humble enough to persistently return to God. To win the battle against evil and sin, we must turn and become like children (see Mt 18:3). Our heavenly Father cannot resist when his children run to him with open arms, begging for his help. God is eager to give us mercy and life-giving grace. In our every choice, God will urge us to set things right so that God might make our souls "white as snow" (Is 1:18). God not only wants to share the joy of the afterlife with us. God wants to share life with us *now*. When we remember death, we also remember that God wants us to "eat the good things of the land" (Is 1:19) and to enjoy a life well-lived.

Examen and Intercessory Prayer

Review your day (see the Memento Mori Daily Examen, p. 8).

Bring to mind someone you know who has trouble believing in God's mercy. Pray a Hail Mary for all those who struggle to accept and believe in the Father's love and mercy.

Think of a beautiful peach with its delicate tint of rose, with its flavor so sweet that no human skill could invent such nectar. Tell me . . . is it for the peach's own sake that God created that color so fair to the eye, that velvety covering so soft to the touch? Is it for itself that he made it so sweet? No, it is for us. The only thing that is all its own and is essential to its being is the pit—it possesses nothing beyond.

Thus, also it pleases Jesus to lavish his gifts on certain souls in order to draw still more to himself. In his mercy, he humbles them inwardly and gently compels them to recognize their nothingness and his almighty power. Now this sentiment of humility is like a kernel of grace which God hastens to develop against that blessed day, when, clothed with an imperishable beauty, they will be placed, without danger, on the banquet table of paradise. . . .

I am not always faithful, but I never lose courage. I leave myself in the arms of Our Lord. He teaches me to draw profit from everything, from the good and the bad that he finds in me. He teaches me to invest in the Bank of Love, or rather it is he who invests for me, without telling me how he does it—that is his affair, not mine. I have but to surrender myself entirely to him, to do so without reserve, without even the satisfaction of knowing what it will bring to me.

—Saint Thérèse of Lisieux, *Letter 16 to Céline*

Journaling and Prayer

Take some time to picture the grace of God washing your soul, making it white as snow. Reflect on how God's grace has changed your life.

Draw a picture or a symbol of a humble heart. Or write a prayer asking God for humility.

Wednesday

READINGS: JER 18:18–20 / PS 31:5–6, 14, 15–16 / MT 20:17–28

"The Son of Man did not come to be served but to serve and to give his life as a ransom for many."

—Matthew 20:28

IN TODAY'S GOSPEL, JESUS takes aside the twelve Apostles and gives them a detailed account of the future. He tells them that he will be condemned, handed over to the Gentiles, mocked, scourged, and that he will rise on the third day. Jesus' astounding revelation contradicts many of the Apostles' expectations for the Messiah they had so long awaited. One might think that after hearing Jesus' words, the Apostles would have taken the opportunity to reflect and let them sink in. Instead, many did what we all do when we hear something we do not want to hear—they pretended they had not heard it.

After Jesus' revelation, James and John approach Jesus with their mother. Mute and cowardly, they allow their mother to voice the human motivations that often lie beneath and make murky even the best of intentions. She proceeds to ask Jesus boldly that her sons sit at his right and left in his new kingdom. Since only two people can sit at Jesus' right and left, James and John are asking for the most coveted roles—at the expense of their friends. James and John have just heard the news that their Master will die a terrible death and rise on the third day. Astonishingly, their response is to allow their mother to voice the selfish thought foremost in their minds, "What's in it for me?"

The battle between life and death rages in our hearts, and we give into death every time we hear the Good News of the Gospel and ask, "What's in it for me?" Of course, Jesus did promise his followers that they would receive "a hundred times more" in this life *and* "eternal life in the age to come" (Mk 10:30). Great rewards are involved when we follow Jesus. But we cannot follow him wholeheartedly and remain self-centered. Remembering death helps us to combat a selfish mindset that is neither truly useful nor holy. Had James and John remembered that they would die, they likely would have prioritized good and holy goals over earthly power. Similarly, when we remember our death it recontextualizes our selfish desires and helps us to realize what is truly in our best interest.

Examen and Intercessory Prayer

Review your day (see the Memento Mori Daily Examen, p. 8).

Think of anyone you have hurt because you acted out of selfish motivations. Say a Hail Mary for these people and make amends if you are able.

> I hope you won't be negligent about your prayers. You know death soon takes us, and often unawares, from the greatest pleasures this world can bestow. . . . Don't forget to say prayers . . . for a happy death. We ought, you know, to take a little trouble to prepare for that which should be the concern of our whole life. Oh, my dear ones, when we consider how soon death will cut us off, we ought to forget everything, to gain the one thing necessary. . . . Meditate particularly on the miseries of this life, so that you may not be too taken up with its pleasures. Meditate often on death also, so that you may not be attached to this life; and on the shortness of time, that it may prepare you for eternity. Eternity is endless. . . . We should make good use of the few moments God gives us here!
>
> —Saint Elizabeth Ann Seton

Journaling and Prayer

Reflect on a time that you were more concerned about honors and personal benefit than with following Jesus.

Write a prayer to Jesus asking him to help you purify your motivations as you follow him.

Thursday

Readings: Jer 17:5–10 / Ps 1:1–2, 3, 4, 6 / Lk 16:19–31

"Then Abraham said, 'If they will not listen to Moses and the prophets, neither will they be persuaded if someone should rise from the dead.'"

—Luke 16:31

WHEN WE REMEMBER DEATH we also remember that our actions have consequences in the afterlife. The rich man in today's Gospel almost certainly did not consider life after death when he continually passed by poor Lazarus lying at his front gate. Perhaps the rich man knew that his actions would have consequences in the afterlife but chose to ignore them. But fear of the after-life should not have been what motivated the rich man to be good to Lazarus. He should have treated Lazarus with love because he loved God. Had the rich man known God and lived for God, he never would have passed by poor Lazarus without wanting to help him. If the rich man had known God, he would have seen God in Lazarus.

Remembering the afterlife helps us to make fruitful, good choices in the everyday moments of life. However, if remembering the afterlife leads us to live only in trembling fear of hell, then our gaze is focused in the wrong direction. We think of the afterlife not in order to fear hell but to remember our goal: eternal life. God wants to save us and he has saved us through our Baptism. We have only to continue to accept his grace and to trust in God's deep and abiding love. If we find it difficult to trust in God's love, we can constantly turn these doubts over to Jesus. God's love is absolutely indubitable. Like a raging gale or a colossal tsunami, God's love is far fiercer and unyielding than our fears and doubts.

When we allow God to love us, this love energizes our lives and prepares us for the afterlife. Living for heaven will not make us somber saints, but holy people full of zeal and joy. If the rich man had lived for heaven, both his life on earth and his afterlife would have been filled with this joy. Unlike the rich man, we still have the opportunity to accept God's love in order to love others more fully. When we remember our death, we are invited to live for heaven by choosing this love every day. Rather than filling us with fear, the thought of death helps us to be persuaded by God's love and to live in a way that demonstrates our transformation in Christ.

Examen and Intercessory Prayer

Review your day (see the Memento Mori Daily Examen, p. 8).

Have you ever passed by a Lazarus without looking that person in the eye and respecting his or her dignity? Place these people in the hands of God as you pray a Hail Mary for their intentions.

> Live well, that you may not die ill. . . . Remember the rich and the poor man in the Gospel? . . . The poor man died and was carried by the angels into Abraham's bosom. The rich man also died and was buried in hell. And being in torment he lifted up his eyes and saw Lazarus resting in Abraham's bosom. Then he cried, saying, "Father Abraham, have mercy on me, and send Lazarus that he may dip his finger in water, and drop it on my tongue, for I am tormented in this flame." Proud in the world, in hell a beggar! . . . Of these two, tell me, which died well, and which died ill? Do not ask the eyes, return to the heart. For if you ask the eyes, they will answer you falsely. For vastly splendid, and disguised with much worldly show, are the honors that must have been paid to the rich man in his death. What crowds of mourning servants must have been there! What pompous train of family members and friends! What splendid funeral proceedings! What a costly burial! I assume [his body] was overwhelmed with spices. What shall we say then, did he die well or die ill? If you ask the eyes, he died very well; if you ask your inner Master, he died most ill.
>
> If haughty men who keep their own goods to themselves, and bestow none of them upon the poor, die in

this way, how will those who plunder the goods of others die? Therefore I have said with true reason, "Live well, that you do not die ill, that you die not as that rich man died." . . . Have respect for the poor, whether lying on the ground, or walking; have respect for the poor, do good works. Let the number of those who do good works increase; since the number of the faithful increases also.

—Saint Augustine, *Sermon 52 on the New Testament*

Journaling and Prayer

Think of a day when you lived as one who is persuaded by the truth of Jesus Christ. Imagine that day and enter into it in your mind. Thank God for the gift of that day and ask him to give you the grace to live more days like it.

Write a prayer to Jesus asking him to fill your heart with love and compassion for everyone you meet.

Friday

READINGS: Gn 37:3–4, 12–13a, 17b–28a / Ps 105:16–17, 18–19, 20–21 /
Mt 21:33–43, 45–46

For God so loved the world that he gave his only Son,
so that everyone who believes in him might not perish
but might have eternal life.

—John 3:16

EVERY PERSON WANTS TO be unique and appreciated for
who she is when held against the background of the
rest of humanity. We want to surround ourselves with
people who understand us and make us feel strikingly
exceptional. For this reason, many of us join "tribes"
according to our backgrounds, musical tastes, or favorite sports teams. We search for people who appreciate
the same things, hoping they will appreciate us too.
Once we've found our clique, we use our membership in
the exclusive group to elevate ourselves above others.

We act as if we are above the trends, the obsessions, and the unimportant dramas of the ordinary world.

Many of us behave similarly when it comes to our religious beliefs. We subconsciously want our religious beliefs to be as unique, unmatchable, and distinct as we are. As a result, some people reject the Gospel simply because so many others accept it. Some embrace the faith but live to separate themselves from the unity of the Church. If we are honest with ourselves, most of us will recognize some way in which antipathy against the simple, unifying beauty of the Gospel message simmers in our hearts. For example, we might treat today's Gospel verse, John 3:16, like white noise. It conveys the simplicity of the Gospel message in one line, but we prefer to hear something more unexpected. We might even resist reflecting on this verse because we think we know what it means. We have heard this passage a million times; so many times that the words might cause us to cringe. But unlike many of the actually tiresome and overdone things in this world, the rich and profound depth of the Gospel can never be completely plumbed.

John 3:16 is often painted on signs and waved at protests and sports events because it contains the depth of the entire Gospel. Rather than ignore it because it is overused, we are called to allow this line to shock us anew each time we read it. Jesus died to save us from death. But we often forget to plunge our lives into the alarming and consoling context of eternal life. We lose sight of Jesus and get lost in ordinary daily realities. We obsess about the things that should truly bore us: TV shows, dramas on social media, gossip, political scandals, and fights among family and friends. We drown in the chaos of the mundane. The really tiresome things in life begin to consume us while we ignore the jewels of the Gospel. Remembering death daily can change that. With the grace of God, we can learn daily to be bored by the things that should bore us and to find life in Life itself.

Examen and Intercessory Prayer

Review your day (see the Memento Mori Daily Examen, p. 8).

Pray for yourself that you can view all things in life according to God's truth. Pray a Hail Mary for your increase in holiness.

From what source did God so love the world? From no other source than from his own goodness. Now, let us be abashed at his love, let us be ashamed at the excess of his loving kindness, since he spared not his only-begotten Son for our sakes. . . . He gave us his own Son, but for him we do not so much as despise money, not even for ourselves. And how can these things deserve pardon? If we see a man submitting to sufferings and death for us, we set him before all others, count him among our chief friends, place in his hands all that is ours, and deem it his rather than our own. Even so, do not imagine that we give him the return that he deserves. . . . He laid down his life for us, and poured forth his precious Blood for our sake, we who were neither well-disposed nor good. In the meantime, we do not even pour out our money for our own [spiritual well-being], and we neglect him who died for us, when he is naked and a stranger. . . . But why speak just of money? Had we ten thousand lives, should we not lay them all down for him?

—Saint John Chrysostom, *Homily 27 on the Gospel of John*

Journaling and Prayer

Reflect on what it would look like to plunge your life into the context of eternal life—to truly live your life in view of what comes after death.

Letter your favorite Scripture passage. Take some time to deeply reflect on it. Explore its many layers of meaning and give thanks to God for his Word.

Saturday

READINGS: Mɪ 7:14–15, 18–20 / Pѕ 103:1–2, 3–4, 9–10, 11–12 /
Lᴋ 15:1–3, 11–32

"Let us celebrate with a feast, because this son of mine was dead, and has come to life again; he was lost, and has been found."

—Luke 15:23–24

Wʜᴀᴛ ɪᴍᴀɢᴇѕ ᴄᴏᴍᴇ ᴛᴏ mind when you think of death? Perhaps gravestones, coffins, or skulls? Certainly, these are signs of physical death, but there is another kind of death. While bodily death is inevitable, another avoidable death holds far more danger. In today's Gospel, when the father of the prodigal son says that his son was dead, he is not speaking poetically. Rather, he describes his son's condition more honestly than had he been standing over his son's grave. The Book of Revelation calls this kind of death the "second death," referring not to the natural death of the body but to the death of the soul through sin (see 20:6, 20:14–15, 21:8).

The death of sin is far more hazardous than natural death. Some of us know this intellectually, but often we do not believe it deeply enough to make radical changes in our lives. Like the prodigal son, we wander to far-off lands searching for something—anything—that might give us fulfillment. We reject our loving Father and search elsewhere for life. In an effort to grasp immortality, we put our trust in anti-aging creams, money saved in bank vaults, or knowledge stored in our minds. We fool ourselves into believing that super-ficial things can give us more life than dying to sin. In short, we often fear bodily death much more than we fear the death of sin. Meanwhile, our Father in heaven waits for us, loves us, and wants so much to give us everything he has.

Our God has power over life and death. Jesus died for us and has given us the life-giving grace of salvation—this is all we really need. Christ has opened the doors of heaven. We should not fear the death of our bodies. Rather, we should fear the most definitive evil and the most dangerous death: sin. We should spend our time energetically avoiding and dreading sin, not physical death. Sin should terrify us much more than skulls, graves, and coffins. Lord, save us from this death!

Examen and Intercessory Prayer

Review your day (see the Memento Mori Daily Examen, p. 8).

Pray a Hail Mary for all those who put their trust in something or someone other than God.

Most high, all powerful, all good Lord!
All praise is yours, all glory, all honor, and all blessing.

To you, alone, Most High, do they belong.
No mortal lips are worthy to pronounce your name.

Be praised, my Lord, through all your creatures,
especially through my lord Brother Sun,
who brings the day; and you give light through him.
And he is beautiful and radiant in all his splendor!
Of you, Most High, he bears the likeness.

Be praised, my Lord, through Sister Moon and the stars;
in the heavens you have made them bright, precious,
    and beautiful.

Be praised, my Lord, through Brothers Wind and Air,
and clouds and storms, and all the weather,
through which you give your creatures sustenance.

Be praised, my Lord, through Sister Water;
she is very useful and humble and precious and pure.

Be praised, my Lord, through Brother Fire,
through whom you brighten the night.
He is beautiful and cheerful and powerful and strong.

Be praised, my Lord, through our sister Mother Earth,
who feeds us and rules us,
and produces various fruits with colored flowers
    and herbs.

Be praised, my Lord, through those who forgive for love
  of you;
through those who endure sickness and trial.

Happy are those who endure in peace,
for by you, Most High, they will be crowned.

Be praised, my Lord, through our Sister Bodily Death,
from whose embrace no living person can escape.

Woe to those who die in mortal sin!
Happy are those she finds doing your most holy will.
The second death can do no harm to them.

Praise and bless my Lord, and give thanks,
and serve him with great humility.

     —Saint Francis of Assisi, *The Canticle of the Sun*

Journaling and Prayer

What gives you life—not the "life" that comes from the superficial, passing things of this world—but true life that participates in God who is Life? Reflect on how you can integrate more life-giving activities into your daily life.

Write about or draw an experience that helped you to feel close to God's life.

Third Week of Lent

Saint Jerome Reading, Georges de la Tour.

Sunday

Scrutiny Readings: Ex 17:3–7 / Ps 95:1–2, 6–7, 8–9 / Rom 5:1–2, 5–8 / Jn 4:5–42

> Jesus answered and said to her, "If you knew the gift of God and who is saying to you, 'Give me a drink,' you would have asked him and he would have given you living water."
>
> —John 4:10

Jesus' exchange with the Samaritan woman in today's Gospel is rich and unexpected. He enters the woman's life suddenly, like a tidal wave. Barely a few sentences into the conversation, Jesus points out that the woman has had five husbands. The reason the Samaritan woman had five husbands is unknown. It could have been due to death, promiscuity, abuse, or a combination of these things. Regardless, Jesus seemed to know that, by necessity or choice, the woman had rooted much of her identity in other people. He immediately points this out as an obstacle to her relationship with God.

We all have tried at one time or another to find fulfillment or security in other human beings. We naturally look to external things to slake our thirst for love. Perhaps we expect more from a friend or significant other than that person can give. Or we meet someone or something happens and we believe our problems are solved, our empty hearts forever filled. But disappointment always awaits. The *Catechism of the Catholic Church* tells us, "the desire for God is written in the human heart" (no. 27). Yet, like the Samaritan woman, we try to fill our hearts with something or someone who will only end up disappointing us. Even the faithful love of a spouse, family members, and friends cannot completely fulfill us. No one but God can quench our thirst with living water, because no one but God created us. No one but God sustains us in life. No one but God can accompany us in death and bring us to eternal life. Deep down we know this, but we still search for and cling to other people and things. We remain skeptical.

When Jesus offered the Samaritan woman "living water," she too was skeptical. Experienced in the art of the search for meaning, she knew that her search for love had always led to disappointment. But as she talks to Jesus, she realizes that he is the One for whom she has always searched. Jesus Christ is the only person who can fill her heart. The living water that Jesus offers the woman is himself. Through Baptism, Jesus becomes in us "a spring of water welling up into eternal life" (Jn 1:14). When we feel thirsty, unloved, or fearful of death, we can remember that we are filled with the living waters of Christ. And this living water will carry us through death—a mere passageway—into eternal life.

Examen and Intercessory Prayer

Review your day (see the Memento Mori Daily Examen, p. 8).

Think of a person you know who is estranged from family. Say a Hail Mary for all broken relationships, couples on the brink of divorce, and all families in need of special graces.

> We see the true value of things by the light of eternity. Oh, how empty is all that has not been done for God and with God! I beg you to mark all your doings with the seal of love; it is the only thing that lasts! . . . What a serious thing life is! Each minute is given us for the purpose of rooting ourselves more deeply in God, according to Saint Paul's expression [see Col 2:7], so that we may attain a more striking likeness to our Master, a closer union. The secret of realizing this plan, formed by God himself, is to forget, to forsake self, no longer making any account of it; to look upon the divine Master and on him alone; to receive joy or sorrow indifferently, as both coming from his love. This establishes the soul upon the summits where all is peace.
>
> —Saint Elizabeth of the Trinity, *Letter 333*

Journaling and Prayer

How are you like the Samaritan woman? Where do you search for meaning outside of the waters of eternal life?

Write a prayer to Jesus, asking him to help you to remain in the waters of eternal life welling up in your soul.

Monday

READINGS: 2 KG 5:1–15 / PS 42:2–3; 43:3, 4 / LK 4:24–30

> The king of Israel tore his garments and exclaimed: "Am I a god with power over life and death, that this man should send someone for me to cure him of leprosy?"
>
> —2 Kings 5:7

DESPERATE FOR A CURE, Naaman went to the king of Israel to seek healing from his leprosy. Though Naaman associated power over life and death with earthly power, the king of Israel knew the limits of his authority. He knew that only God has power over life and death. So, upon hearing that Naaman wanted to be healed, the king assumed it was a trap and tore his garments in distress. But Israel's prophet Elisha was undisturbed. He knew that he could heal Naaman—not because he had the power but because God shares his power. While the king had little faith, Elisha knew that God is so powerful he can heal others in any way God chooses. Believing in God's immense power, Elisha told Naaman to bathe in the Jordan seven times. Elisha trusted that God could heal through him—a fallible, finite human being—and a simple ritual involving material things.

Naaman's healing foreshadowed the gift of the Sacraments. Saint Thomas Aquinas wrote: "Water flowed from Christ's side to wash us; blood to redeem us" (*STh* III, q. 66, a. 3). Jesus instituted the sacraments through the power of the Cross using material things and fallible people as the primary source of his saving power in the world. The power always resides in God, but he extends his life-giving graces to us through humble means. Priests consecrate the Eucharist and give absolution in the sacrament of Reconciliation. Water bathes us in Baptism. Chrism oil in Confirmation anoints our foreheads and our soul. Bread and wine turn into Christ's Body and Blood. God uses the least likely materials and instruments to pour out saving grace on us.

We may be powerless over life and death but we believe in a Savior who is Victor over death. However, like Naaman, sometimes we reject the idea that God can work through simple people, rituals, and materials. We want God to do something greater, something more unusual—we expect a show. We avoid frequenting the sacraments because they may seem useless, simple, and ordinary. But when we think in this way, like Naaman, our pride prevents us from seeking healing. In the waters of Baptism, in the Eucharist, and in the words of absolution, we are cured not of leprosy but of a far more dangerous illness that can lead to permanent death:

sin. We are incapable of healing sin's terminal illness, but we do not have to rend our garments in distress. God has saved us. We have done nothing to deserve this healing, this life. But God wants to give it to us anyway in the most ordinary and unexpected ways. Jesus died to give us life. We need only accept God's mysterious ways and walk into the flowing, healing waters of grace.

Examen and Intercessory Prayer

Review your day (see the Memento Mori Daily Examen, p. 8).

Write a list of people and places in the world that need healing. Pray a Hail Mary for these intentions.

Anima Christi

Soul of Christ, sanctify me.
Body of Christ, save me.
Blood of Christ, cleanse me.
Water from the side of Christ, wash me.
Passion of Christ, strengthen me.
Good Jesus, hear me.
Within your wounds hide me.
Never let me be parted from you.
From the evil one protect me.
In the hour of my death, call me
and bid me come to you,
that with your saints I may praise you
forever and ever. Amen.

—An anonymous fourteenth-century prayer

Journaling and Prayer

Identify an area or areas in your life where you need healing. Write a list if it is helpful. Ask the Lord for the healing you need with the trust that he will pour his life-giving grace into your life in countless, unexpected ways.

Draw a picture of your Baptism. Or write a prayer of trust in God.

Tuesday

READINGS: DN 3:25, 34–43 / PS 25:4–5AB, 6, 7BC, 8, 9 / MT 18:21–35

"Lord, if my brother sins against me, how often must I forgive him? As many as seven times?"

—Matthew 18:21

PEOPLE CAN BE IRRITATING, OFFENSIVE, abusive, or just downright intolerable. All of us have been affected by another person's inappropriate or even evil behavior, so we can relate to Peter's question in today's Gospel. Peter reasonably asks Jesus how many times he has to forgive another person, and he gives a pretty generous possibility. Jesus responds with a seemingly unreasonable answer. Seventy seven times! In other words, Jesus insists that the Christian can never cease forgiving.

To be Christian is to live in continual forgiveness. However, Jesus' teaching to repeatedly forgive can be misunderstood. He is not imparting easily dismissed, superficial, pop-psychology platitudes. Neither is he suggesting that we allow abusive people to harm us. We do not have to act as doormats or pretend we don't have needs. Jesus wants us to love ourselves as he loves us. Instead, with his injunction to forgive always, Jesus points to the deeper reality of the Trinity. Relationship is key to the spiritual life because God is Three Persons. The Trinity—a unified, dynamic relationship—is the source of all other life. Relationship, therefore, is life. And rupture in relationship is death.

However, human relationships and connections are not divine. We cannot expect perfect love from others. Although every human being is made in God's image, our actions do not always reflect that dignity. We are broken by sin, which leads to broken relationships. So, if a person chooses to rupture a relationship with inappropriate or even evil behavior, we do not necessarily have to continue to be in relationship with them. But we do have one responsibility: to forgive. Forgiveness repairs our relationships with other people, if possible. And if not, forgiveness frees our hearts to be in relationship with God.

Remembrance of death can motivate us to allow God to clear grudges, anger, and a desire for retaliation from our souls. Since we may die at any time, we must search our hearts daily to root out unforgiveness. The life-giving graces of the sacraments make possible the difficult task of continual forgiveness. When we receive them, we can ask God to clear the remnants of unforgiveness that linger in our hearts. Ultimately, God is the one who gives us the power to forgive, and we do so not only for others' sake but primarily for our own spiritual well-being. Forgiveness helps us to grow in union with God who has forgiven us so much. Forgiveness heals relationships, if possible, but most importantly our souls. Forgiveness clears away what stands in the way of our union with God's life.

Examen and Intercessory Prayer

Review your day (see the Memento Mori Daily Examen, p. 8).

Think of several difficult people in your life. Pray a Hail Mary that you might discern how and whether to be in relationship with these people. Pray also for forgiveness no matter what happens.

> A young man, who had not long been under Saint Philip Neri's direction, could not be persuaded to forgive an injury which he had received. Philip did all he could to induce the youth, but his heart seemed only to harden more. One day, finding no other means that worked, Philip took up a crucifix and said to the youth with great fervor, "Look at this, and think how much Blood our Lord has shed for love of you. And he not only pardoned his enemies, but prayed that the Eternal Father would pardon them also. Do you not see, my poor child, that every day when you say the *Pater Noster*, instead of asking pardon for your sins, you are calling down vengeance upon yourself?" He then told the youth to kneel down at the foot of the crucifix which he held before him. Then he told the youth to repeat a prayer after him in which Philip magnified the

hardness and obstinacy of the youth's heart and showed him what a grievous sin he was committing. The youth knelt down and tried to repeat the prayer, but began to tremble all over and could not pronounce a word. He remained a long time in this state, but at last getting up exclaimed, "Here I am, Father, ready to obey you; I pardon every injury I have ever received!"

—Pietro Giacamo Bocci, *The Life of Saint Philip Neri*

Journaling and Prayer

Reflect on your ability (or inability) to forgive. Think of times when you have been able, with God's grace, to forgive someone in a heroic way. Thank God for the times you have been able to forgive, and ask God to help you in relationships that continue to be difficult.

Write down a list of people you need to forgive. Burn the list and, as you burn it, pray, "I forgive (name) in the grace of Jesus Christ."

Wednesday

Readings: Dt 4:1, 5–9 / Ps 147:12–13, 15–16, 19–20 / Mt 5:17–19

Hear the statutes and ordinances I am teaching you to observe, that you may live.

—Deuteronomy 4:1

LIKE ADAM AND EVE, HUMANITY continues to believe the serpent who assures us, "You certainly will not die!" (Gen 3:4). We naturally chafe against rules dictating specific behavior, even God's rules. We demand that God not interfere with anything we desire to do with our free will, our bodies, and our lives. We eat the fruit of the tree simply because we don't like being told what to do, and we choose to believe there will be no consequences. This temptation to rebellion is familiar to every human who has ever walked the earth. And since the beginning of time, every generation falls prey to the temptation to believe that God's law is unnecessary and disposable.

Our modern world continues to sing the age-old refrain of sin: "Rules kill and the absence of rules brings life!" Like every falsehood, this message has a seed of truth, which is why it successfully confuses so many people. At some point, we all have bought this lie because we know that some human-made rules can kill. Many of Jesus' actions communicated this truth. Jesus was constantly "breaking the rules" to perform his ministry, something that infuriated the scribes and Pharisees and led them to plot his death. However, Jesus also declared, "Do not think that I have come to abolish the law or the prophets. I have come not to abolish but to fulfill" (Mt 5:17). In a time when rules are progressively discarded with more and more frequency, Jesus' words urge caution. We cannot assume we know which rules can be carelessly cast aside.

According to Saint Thomas Aquinas, "every knowledge of truth is a kind of reflection and participation of the eternal law, which is the unchangeable truth" (*STh*, I–II. q. 92. a. 2). Knowledge of the truth helps us to understand what we should and should not do. God is Truth, so his law is first rooted in God's very identity. Jesus could distinguish between the law and useless rules because he was measuring it against himself, who is Truth. We cannot do the same because we are not God. But Jesus dwells now in the Body of Christ, the Church. We can trust the Church to continue to faithfully and truthfully transmit God's law to us through the ages because Jesus Truth dwells within it. The indwelling of the Trinity present within us through our Baptism also helps us to follow and to discern God's law. In our every discernment, however, it is always important to remember that the law derives not from our own feelings, thoughts, and preferences, but from God who is unchangeable Truth.

In the Christian tradition, *memento mori* is a practice that necessarily involves living in God's life-giving presence and following God's law. In fact, remembrance of death is absolutely useless if a person were to choose not to live according to God's law and to continue in the death of sin. After all, what use is remembering death if we do not live for heaven? Our sinfulness may tempt us to believe that living according to God's law is too constraining and difficult, and certainly it is not always easy. But following this path does lead to happiness in this life and in the next. Therefore, let us act in the presence of our saving God. Let us live according to God's law, not out of fear but out of love for the source of this law: the One who dwells in our soul through Baptism. As we walk with God we will find that, rather than leading to death, this way leads to fruitfulness, healing, and life.

Examen and Intercessory Prayer

Review your day (see the Memento Mori Daily Examen, p. 8).

Think of someone you know who struggles with Church teaching (it may be you). Pray a Hail Mary that the Spirit may guide those who wrestle with Church teaching to understanding and peace.

Without God's assisting grace, the law is the letter that kills. But when the life-giving spirit is present, the law [is] loved as written within. . . . It is evident, then, that

the oldness of the letter, in the absence of the newness of the spirit, instead of freeing us from sin, rather
makes us guilty through the knowledge of sin. As it is
written in another part of Scripture, he that increases
knowledge, increases sorrow [see Ecc 1:18]. Not that
the law itself is evil, but because the commandment
has its good in the acting out of the letter, not in the
assistance of the spirit. And if this commandment is
kept from fear of punishment and not from love of righteousness, it is servilely kept, not freely, and therefore
it is not kept at all. For no fruit is good which does not
grow from the root of love. If, however, faith is present
that works by love [see Gal 5:6] then one begins to
delight in the law of God. . . . And this delight is the gift
of the Spirit, not of the letter; even though there is
another law in our members still warring against
the law of the mind. This happens until the old state
is changed, and passes into that newness which
increases from day to day . . . while the grace of God
liberates us from this body of death through Jesus
Christ our Lord.

—Saint Augustine, *On the Spirit and the Letter*

Journaling and Prayer

Recall a situation in which you shared God's law in a
way that killed. Or recall a time when you reacted to the
"rules" of the Church without considering the power of
grace. Reflect on what you have learned and take some
time for prayer, asking God to shed light on your mind.

Draw a picture or letter a quote related to a scriptural
command from God that brings you life.

Thursday

Readings: Jer 7:23–28 / Ps 95:1–2, 6–7, 8–9 / Lk 11:14–23

"Whoever is not with me is against me, and whoever does not gather with me scatters."

—Luke 11:23

Death literally scatters us. All matter is corruptible and we are born into corruptible bodies. When we die, our flesh and organs will fall away from our bones and rot (unless one happens to become an incorrupt saint). Our bones eventually will decompose too, and all that will be left of us is a grave full of dust or fossils. Sin, the death of the soul, also scatters us. Sin ruptures our relationship with God and neighbor. It creates disunity in the soul. Rather than adhering to God, we tear ourselves into pieces by running after a multitude of other desires. We reach out to one thing after another, yet we never find complete satisfaction. We are divided.

Sin scatters us in a deeper and more metaphysically profound way than natural death because it not only impacts our material body but also our immaterial soul. Doctor of the Church, Saint Teresa of Ávila, describes the shocking reality of a soul in a state of sin: "the soul by sinning withdraws from the stream of life, and growing beside a black and fetid pool, can produce nothing but disgusting and unwholesome fruit." How shocking and undesirable! Perhaps because our sins impact our soul and not always our outward appearance, we more easily dismiss them. But when we ignore the ugliness of sin, it creates disorder within us. Sin flings us in many directions and causes us to lose unity within ourselves. This disunity creates ugliness far deeper than superficial appearances.

Remembrance of death in the tradition of the Church is one way that we can begin to bring unity to our being. When we remember our death, we are faced with the reality and treasure of our short life. Our life ends and it also began. We remember that there must be a cause for our existence that has no cause itself. God who is Existence itself gives us life. When we separate ourselves from the source of our existence through sin, the grace of the Cross unites us once again with God. This unification, however, does not happen away from community. Only within the unity of the Body of Christ do we find unity with God. The Church heals us and unites our divided souls to God. As a mother gives her children the milk of life, the Church too gives us grace. When we remember death, we also remember and give thanks for the source of our existence and the source of our salvation—God.

Examen and Intercessory Prayer

Review your day (see the Memento Mori Daily Examen, p. 8).

Think of anyone you know who has recently lost a family member. Pray a Hail Mary for those who mourn the death of loved ones.

> The Church . . . is one and spread abroad far and wide into a multitude by an increase of fruitfulness. As there are many rays of the sun, but one light; and many branches of a tree, but one source of strength based in its tenacious root; and one spring that flows from many streams . . . yet the unity is still preserved in the source. Separate a ray of the sun from its body of light, and its unity does not allow a division of light. Break a branch from a tree—when broken, it will not be able to bud. Cut off a stream from its source, and it dries up. Thus, the Church also shines with the light of the Lord and sheds forth her rays over the whole world, yet it is one light which is everywhere diffused and the unity of the body is not separated. Her fruitful abundance spreads her branches over the whole world. She broadly expands her rivers, liberally flowing, yet her head is one, her source one. And she is one mother, plentiful in the results of fruitfulness—from her womb we are born, by her milk we are nourished, by her spirit we are animated.
>
> —Saint Cyprian of Carthage, *On the Unity of the Church*

Journaling and Prayer

Pray in thanksgiving for the nourishment of the sacraments in the Church. If you have not received the sacraments in a long time, take some time to pray and ask God to help you to understand more deeply why you need them.

Draw a picture of a headstone for your grave and choose a Scripture quote to go beneath your name. Or write a prayer asking the Lord to help you to die in a state of grace.

Friday

READINGS: Hos 14:2–10 / Ps 81:6c–8a, 8bc–9, 10–11ab, 14 and 17 / Mk 12:28–34

> Straight are the paths of the LORD, the just walk in them, but sinners stumble in them.
>
> —Hosea 14:10

THOUGH IT MAY SEEM difficult to walk in the way of the Lord, today's readings remind us that the Lord's paths are straight for the just. Of course, even the just find it difficult to walk effortlessly in the paths of the Lord. We are all sinners who inevitably falter and at times collapse. We are especially prone to fall when we lack trust in the power of God's grace. Jesus always extends his hand, ready to keep us from stumbling and to lift us up, but sometimes we prefer to remain in sin. Rather than accept help, we remain on the ground, our faces in the dust.

We close ourselves into a casket when we stumble into serious sin and choose not to get up. Lingering in sin turns us into corpses before our bodies are lowered into the grave. We may appear young, healthy, and beautiful, but it's just a façade, like the makeup that a funeral director paints on a corpse. When this happens, we cannot rise on our own strength. Only God can exhume us from our self-imposed graves. God's grace helps us to avoid stumbling to our death and enables us to do what we could have never done before. Grace changes everything. The sacrament of Reconciliation in particular cleanses and fills us with the beauty and light of true life. It enables us to walk in the paths of the Lord and to love God with all our heart, understanding, and strength, and to love our neighbor as ourselves (see Mk 12:33). All God asks is that we continue to follow in this path no matter how many times we fall. With time, things that were formerly impossible become more effortless with God's help.

Remembrance of death helps us to rise from the dirt of sin when we stumble on the Lord's path. We are naturally tempted to postpone holiness and think, "Tomorrow I will stop sinning in this way!" But if we remember death daily it humbles us and reminds us that we could die at any time. Future plans to stop sinning may prove useless because death may come tomorrow. When we keep this reality in mind, we find stronger motivation to seek God's healing and grace. *Memento mori* reminds us that God wants our happiness *now*, not just later.

Examen and Intercessory Prayer

Review your day (see the Memento Mori Daily Examen, p. 8).

Pray a Hail Mary for anyone receiving the sacrament of Reconciliation for the first time and for those who have been away from the sacrament for many years.

The soul is the life of the body, and God is the life of the soul. Thus, sin kills our soul by separating it from God: "Only the one who sins shall die" [Ez 18:20]. Look at the one who has mortally offended the Lord; the person walks, sees, speaks, and you think the person lives. Ah, what lives is the body; the soul has ceased to live. . . . What difference is there between a corpse and a soul in mortal sin? A corpse has lost the use of all its senses. Is this not a faithful image of the sinner? A dead person no longer sees. Everything ought to strike the eyes of the sinner—the state of his soul, the grave ready to open for him—judgment, hell, eternity; and the sinner sees nothing! The dead no longer hear. Everything speaks to the sinner—conscience, grace, events, ministers of religion—and the sinner hears nothing! The dead are insensible. Neither insults nor honors, nor the admiration of people nor their contempt, can touch them. God moves heaven and earth to reach the sinner; he endeavors to rouse him, sometimes by benefits, sometimes by afflictions; and the sinner remains insensible! The sinner exhales an odor of corruption; the contagion of his scandals spreads death around him, and the infection of his vices makes him an object of horror not to just others, but to angels, and to God. O fatal death! O death which deprives us, not of the life of nature, but of the life of grace; that is to say, of the life of God!

—Saint Ignatius of Loyola, *The Spiritual Exercises*

Journaling and Prayer

Reflect on the times in your life when you lay in a grave of sin and refused to seek the help of the sacraments. Then consider how God helped you rise to new life. Thank God for his never-ending forgiveness and ask him for the grace to always seek his help.

Draw the state of a soul in sin and a soul in the state of grace. Or write a prayer asking God to help you to walk in his straight paths.

Saturday

Readings: Hos 6:1–6 / Ps 51:3–4, 18–19, 20–21ab / Lk 18:9–14

"Everyone who exalts himself will be humbled, and the one who humbles himself will be exalted."

—Luke 18:14

JUST AS A DEAD BODY must be lowered into the ground before God can raise it to new life, we too have to sit on the ground of humility before we can be exalted. Saint Augustine once wrote, "Lift not up yourselves, unless you have first been humbled. For many wish to rise before they have sat down, they wish to appear righteous, before they have confessed that they are sinners." Unfortunately, the human instinct is not to humbly lower ourselves to the ground. We would rather stand up and tower over others. We want to make our power felt. We want to be in control. Jesus saw this kind of destructive pride, the root of all sin, all around him.

His disciples competed and fought with one another for honors (see Mk 10:35–45). The elite and powerful were jealous of his miracle-working and authority (see Jn 11:47). Because the Gospels are full of human beings, they are also full of people standing in their pride rather than sitting in humility.

Unsurprisingly then, in many of his parables, Jesus warns against pride. In today's Gospel, he uses the example of a humble tax collector and a self-righteous Pharisee. Jesus chooses these two strikingly different characters to make a point. Like the Pharisee, some people may dress themselves up in the exterior garb of virtuous actions, but sometimes the least likely of people have the more proper interior attitude of humility. Jesus praises this interior attitude because it is the foundation of holiness. Notably, Jesus does not condemn the Pharisee's religious practices or hold up the tax collector as a paragon of virtue. Rather, he urges his disciples to both strive for virtue like the Pharisee and to remain humble of heart like the tax collector.

Humility—the truthful admission that we need God's help—is absolutely necessary when we remember death. The virtue of humility helps us to see that we need Jesus to raise us on the last day. When we choose instead to elevate ourselves above others, we reject the humility of the Cross and therefore God's exalting grace. In the act of pushing ourselves up, we also push away the grace we need to become holier. Remembrance of death helps us to become more like the tax collector who humbly beat his breast, aware that he needed God's saving help. Nothing can save us from death but the justifying grace of Jesus Christ. Paradoxically, by lowering ourselves in humility like a coffin into a grave, we can be confident that Jesus will then raise us to glorious new life.

Examen and Intercessory Prayer

Review your day (see the Memento Mori Daily Examen, p. 8).

Pray for those who puff themselves up with pride, whether out of narcissism, low self-worth, or a need to be powerful. Pray a Hail Mary that all, including yourself, may grow in humility.

> Pride gives birth to envy right away—she is never without such a daughter and companion. By these two evils—pride and envy—the devil is at work. . . . Therefore, the teacher of humility, Christ, first emptied himself, taking the form of a servant, coming in human likeness, and found in human appearance, he humbled himself, making himself obedient even unto death, even the death of the Cross [see Phil 2:7–8]. . . . When Christ humbled himself even unto death, even the death of the Cross . . . what did he show, save, that he would bestow exaltation to all who first followed him as a teacher of humility? And when he was about to enter his passion, he washed the feet of his disciples, and most openly taught them to do the same for their fellow disciples what he, their Lord and Master, had done for them. . . . Therefore, all Christians should guard humility, for to the extent that it is from Christ they are called Christians.

> —Saint Augustine, *Of Holy Virginity*

Journaling and Prayer

Reflect on the virtue of humility. Have you striven for it, prayed for it, thought of it? Take some time to ask Jesus to help you to follow in his humble footsteps. If you are inspired, end by writing a prayer to God asking to grow in the virtue of humility.

Imagine you are the tax collector in the Temple. Stand before God and allow the humility of truth to well up in your heart. Humbly speak to God and allow God to respond to you. Remain in this imaginative prayer for some time and write down what you experience.

Fourth Week of Lent

Saint Francis in Meditation, Caravaggio.

Sunday

Scrutiny Readings: 1 Sm 16:1b, 6–7, 10–13a / Ps 23:1–3a, 3b–4, 5, 6 / Eph 5:8–14 / Jn 9:1–41

"I am the light of the world."

—John 9:5

In today's Gospel, Jesus declares to a blind man, "I am the light of the world." Upon hearing Jesus' words, the blind man was probably confused. Perhaps he thought that Jesus meant that he did not require healing because Jesus' spiritual light should suffice. But the man soon realized that Jesus is a powerful healing light that shines on both our bodies and souls. Jesus spits on the ground, makes a clay, smears it on the blind man's eyes, and tells him to wash his face. Jesus could not bear to declare to the man that he was the light of the world and then leave him in physical darkness. The Divine Physician wanted the blind man to experience his healing both spiritually and physically.

Like the blind man, all of us are born with imperfect bodies. We might inordinately focus on a slight physical imperfection like a big nose or a few extra pounds, but the greatest imperfection of our bodies is that they tend toward death. No matter how many surgeries we undergo, how much we exercise, or how many vitamins we take, our bodies will break down slowly over time. Indeed, no matter what we do, our bodies will succumb to old age and die. We should try to make healthy choices, but, as bodily death is inevitable, it is far more important to focus on our spiritual health. Youth fades and health deteriorates, but everyone can grow in the beauty of holiness.

Each day when we practice *memento mori*, we remember the shadow of death that constantly threatens to overtake us in this life. But we should also remember that death is no match for the powerful radiance of Jesus Christ that scatters every darkness. We are destined for complete physical and spiritual healing if we continue to follow Christ our Light. In heaven, our resurrected bodies will be light-filled, incapable of suffering, and perfect in every way—both physically and spiritually: "The righteous will shine like the sun in the kingdom of their Father" (Mt 13:43). However, healing is not just in our future. Jesus, the Light of the World, wants to heal us now. When we remember our death, we present ourselves before Jesus like the blind man and ask him to heal us. Jesus may choose to heal us physically, if it is his will, but we can be sure that he always will heal us spiritually. Each day when we face the darkness of death, Jesus fills us with his light.

Examen and Intercessory Prayer

Review your day (see the Memento Mori Daily Examen, p. 8).

Pray for someone you know who is in darkness right now: emotional, moral, or physical. Pray a Hail Mary for all who suffer in darkness.

Had we not known the Word and been illuminated by him we would have been no different from fowls that are being fed, fattened in darkness, and nourished for death. Let us then admit the light, that we may admit God; let us admit the light, and become disciples of the Lord. . . . You lead me to the light, O Lord, and I find God through you, and receive the Father from you. . . . Let us put away oblivion of the truth, namely ignorance. And, removing the darkness that obstructs, as dimness of sight, let us contemplate the one true God, raising our voice in a hymn of praise: "Hail, O light! For in us, buried in darkness, shut up in the shadow of death, light has shone forth from heaven, purer than the sun, sweeter than life here below." That light is eternal life; and whoever partakes of it lives. . . . The Sun of Righteousness drives his chariot over all, and pervades equally all of humanity as his Father makes his sun rise on all and distills on them the dew of truth. He has changed sunset into sunrise, and through the Cross brought death to life; and having wrenched us from destruction, he has raised us to the skies, transplanting mortality into immortality. . . . What, then, is the exhortation I give you? I urge you to be saved. Christ desires this. In one word, he freely bestows life on you. And who is he? Briefly learn. He is the Word of truth, the Word of incorruption, that regenerates us by bringing us back to the truth—the prod that urges to salvation—he who expels destruction and pursues death.

—Saint Clement of Alexandria,
Exhortation to the Heathen

Journaling and Prayer

Imagine that you are the blind man in today's Gospel. Present yourself to Jesus and ask him to heal you. Reflect and pray with the scene for some time. Write down your experience.

Draw a symbol of Christ's light or write a prayer to Christ our Light.

Monday

READINGS: Is 65:17–21 / Ps 30:2, 4, 5–6, 11–12a, 13b / Jn 4:43–54

"You may go; your son will live."

—John 4:50

IN TODAY'S GOSPEL, A ROYAL official approaches Jesus and asks him to go to his house to heal his son. Jesus does not go with him but simply tells the man that his son will be healed. The official believes Jesus, leaves, and finds out later that his son was healed at the moment Jesus spoke. All who witnessed this event saw that Jesus' word heals. That day, the royal official and "his whole household" (Jn 4:53) came to believe that Jesus gives life. They realized that Jesus is so powerful that he can heal with just a word. Christ enters any suffering that strikes humanity and brings life.

Like the royal official, we sometimes ask or even demand that Jesus heal us, our loved ones, and the world. We see suffering and we cry out to God. People we love lose jobs, get cancer, or die suddenly. Prisoners languish in cells. Immigrants sigh in detention centers. Fetuses cry in the womb. The homeless sleep in cardboard boxes. Refugees eke out an existence in squalid camps. The elderly live in loneliness and gloomy solitude. Suffering people cry out for justice, for change, for healing. It is difficult to understand why God seems to not always respond to these cries.

However, we often fail to comprehend that God has already sent us a response to suffering: his Word. The death of suffering, like our own death, is inevitable. The Cross did not immediately eradicate all human suffering, but Jesus has pulled it out at the root. Heaven holds no pain. In the meantime, Jesus has transformed suffering so it no longer has power over us and can actually be used by God for good: "This momentary light affliction is producing for us an eternal weight of glory beyond all comparison" (2 Cor 4:17). Shockingly, the Cross even allows us to embrace suffering because by it we enter into the death and resurrection of Jesus Christ (see Rom 6:5). Suffering never has the final word because "the people who walked in darkness have seen a great light" (Is 9:1).

Examen and Intercessory Prayer

Review your day (see the Memento Mori Daily Examen, p. 8).

Think of people you know who are suffering emotionally and physically. Pray a Hail Mary for those undergoing great suffering in the world today.

I know what is for my benefit. Now I begin to be a disciple. And let nothing visible or invisible prevent me from attaining Jesus Christ. Let fire and the Cross; let the crowds of wild beasts; let tearings, breakings, and dislocations of bones; let cutting off of limbs; let shatterings of the whole body; and let all the dreadful torments of the devil come upon me: only let me attain Jesus Christ. All the pleasures of the world, and all the kingdoms of this earth, will profit me nothing. It is better for me to die on behalf of Jesus Christ, than to reign over all the ends of the earth. . . . My love has been crucified, and there is no fire in me desiring to be fed; but there is within me a water that lives and speaks, saying to me inwardly, "Come to the Father." I have no delight in corruptible food, or in the pleasures of this life. I desire the bread of God, the heavenly bread, the bread of life, which is the flesh of Jesus Christ, the Son of God, from the seed of David and Abraham. And I desire the drink of God, namely his Blood, which is incorruptible love and eternal life.

—Saint Ignatius of Antioch, *Epistle to the Romans* (martyred at the beginning of the second century)

Journaling and Prayer

Reflect on the events in your life that have led you to wrestle with the reality of suffering. Express to God how you felt in those moments. Consider how your point of view has changed over time. How have you allowed God to change it?

The Psalms show us how we can prayerfully express any emotion we have. Write a prayer to God that communicates the pain and confusion you have felt in difficult moments in life.

Tuesday

READINGS: Ez 47:1–9, 12 / Ps 46:2–3, 5–6, 8–9 / Jn 5:1–16

"Do you want to be well?"

—John 5:6

IN TODAY'S GOSPEL, JESUS asks a man who has been ill for thirty-eight years if he wants to be well. At face value, this seems like a ridiculous question. Of course the man wants to be well. What sick person does not want to be made well? However, Jesus is really asking a deeper question, one that refers not only to physical well-being but also to spiritual well-being. Basically, Jesus is telling the man, "If you want to encounter my healing power, you have to desire healing in all aspects of your life." Jesus questions each of us similarly, asking if we too are willing to confront our lives with his healing power in order to be made well.

Jesus wants to constantly heal us with his saving grace, but so often we turn away. We may not even recognize the little things we do here and there—a harsh word, a slammed door, a roll of the eyes, avoiding something or someone we know we should not. And sometimes our behavior is even worse—a porn video, physical violence, deep-seated pride, gluttony, or abuse of another person. We say that we want to prioritize being healed by Jesus, but how we actually spend our time reveals what is most important to us. Our sins—small and big—often take over a larger portion of our days than time devoted to God. Our behavior constantly belies priorities that, if we are honest with ourselves, are not in line with trying to grow in good health spiritually.

When we think in terms of sin, especially the ones we struggle with most, Jesus' question becomes much less ridiculous. Do we really want to be made well? We certainly don't act like it sometimes. At least the man who had been sick for thirty-eight years knew that he was sick. He knew that he needed help. Some of us won't even admit or are completely incapable of seeing that we are ill. We may say, "Of course I want to be made well!" But in the meantime, we might also refuse to admit how sin is present in our lives. Or sometimes we do realize our sin, but we do not believe in Jesus' powerful forgiveness. We believe in our sins more than in Jesus.

When we remember death, we also remember what Jesus did to save us. This helps us to accept the healing love of Christ more deeply into our hearts. Every time we do this, we say, "Yes Lord, I want to be made well!" We respond "yes" every time we receive the Eucharist and go to confession. We respond "yes" every time reminders of death help us to choose holiness over convenience, pleasure, or sloth. God does not want death to win in our hearts. God wants to pour his healing forgiveness into our hearts. God wants to heal us. But first we have to answer Jesus' question.

Examen and Intercessory Prayer

Review your day (see the Memento Mori Daily Examen, p. 8).

Pray a Hail Mary for all sinners who do not realize the depth of their sin, including yourself.

Death was wound closely to the body and was ruling over it as though united to it [so] it was necessary that life also should be wound closely to the body, so that the body . . . should cast off corruption. . . . For this reason, the Savior put on a body, so that the body, becoming wound closely to his Life, would no longer abide in mortal death. But, having put on immortality, it should from then on rise again and remain immortal. For, once [the body] had put on corruption, it could not rise again unless it put on life. And death likewise from its very nature, could not appear, save in the body. Therefore, [Jesus] put on a body, that he might find death in the body, and blot it out. For how could the Lord have been proved at all to be the Life, had he not quickened what was mortal? . . . If death had been kept from the body by a mere command on his part, the body would nonetheless have been mortal and corruptible, according to the nature of bodies. But, that this should not be, the body put on the incorporeal Word of God, and thus no longer fears either death or corruption, for life is its garment.

—Saint Athanasius, *On the Incarnation of the Word*

Journaling and Prayer

Take some time to pray with and to write your answer to Jesus' question: "Do you want to be well?"

Write down your reflections from your examen. Consider bringing them with you to the sacrament of Reconciliation next time you go.

Wednesday

READINGS: Is 49:8–15 / Ps 145:8–9, 13cd–14, 17–18 / Jn 5:17–30

"Do not be amazed at this, because the hour is coming in which all who are in the tombs will hear his voice and will come out."

—John 5:28

IN TODAY'S GOSPEL, JESUS tells us that one day people in their tombs will hear his voice and come out. This paints a rather terrifying image of the Second Coming: billions of gravesites bursting open, bones rushing together, and formerly dead people bouncing out of their tombs. One might assume that an intense scene like the one Jesus describes would be a singular event like the Second Coming. However, Jesus may have been referring to multiple events in this passage.

In the Gospel of Matthew, the evangelist describes a similar scene right after Jesus dies: "The earth quaked, rocks were split, tombs were opened, and the bodies of many saints who had fallen asleep were raised" (27:51–52). Although debatable, this passage seems to suggest that several people burst from their graves in Jerusalem at the moment of Jesus' death. That some of the saints would have been raised from the dead before Jesus' resurrection seems odd, but it makes sense in light of Saint Paul's assertion that Jesus' *death* destroyed death (see Heb 2:14). In other words, the effects of the Cross were immediate. On an elemental level, nothing in the world would be as it was before Jesus' death. God died in his humanity and conquered death. And for a moment, the world recognizes this radical change—the earth trembles, rocks split, and some of Jerusalem's dead burst from their tombs.

Propelled by the grace and wonder of the Cross, the early resurrections in Jerusalem foreshadow our own final resurrection from the dead. They give us a mere glimpse of what is to come on that day when "the trumpet will sound, the dead will be raised incorruptible, and we shall be changed" (1 Cor 15:52).

When we meditate on our death, we also can reflect on our bodily resurrection on the last day. The two events are inextricably related. Just like the people who burst from their tombs in Jerusalem, we too believe that we will burst from our tombs on the last day to be reunited with our souls in heaven. Meditation on death is also a contemplation of this glorious, shocking future.

Examen and Intercessory Prayer

Review your day (see the Memento Mori Daily Examen, p. 8).

Think of any friends or family members who have passed away. Pray a Hail Mary for all the souls in purgatory.

Behold, all you people, these new wonders! They suspended him on the tree who stretches out the earth. They transfixed him with nails who laid firm the foundation of the world. They circumscribed him who circumscribed the heavens. They bound him who absolves sinners. They gave him vinegar to drink who has made them to drink of righteousness. They fed him with gall who has offered them the Bread of Life. They caused corruption to come upon his hands and feet, who healed their hands and feet. They violently closed his eyes who restored sight to them. They gave him over to the tomb, who raised their dead to life both in the time before his Passion and also while he was hanging on the tree.

For when our Lord was suffering upon the Cross, the tombs were burst open, the infernal region was disclosed, souls leapt forth, the dead returned to life, and many of them were seen in Jerusalem, while the mystery of the Cross was being perfected. . . . Our Lord trampled upon death, dissolved the enmity, bound the strong man, and raised the trophy of the Cross, his body being lifted upon it, that the body might appear on high, and death be trodden underfoot. Then the heavenly powers wondered, the angels

were astonished, the elements trembled, every crea-
ture was shaken while they looked on this new
mystery, and the terrific spectacle that was being
enacted in the universe. . . .

In the Passion of Christ all things were disturbed
and convulsed. The Lord exclaimed, as once before to
Lazarus, "Come forth, you dead, from your tombs and
your secret places; for I, the Christ, give to you resurrection." . . . What is at length this wonderful mystery?
. . . if you should give but one little word, at that instant
all bodies would stand before you.

—Saint Alexander of Alexandria, *Epistles on Arianism*

Journaling and Prayer

At the time of Jesus' death, the Blessed Mother was
perhaps the only disciple who was confident that her
son would rise again. Say a prayer to the Blessed
Mother asking her to intercede for you that you may
increase in faith.

Sister Carly Paula Arcella, FSP, refers to the manner
with which she will burst from her grave at the Second
Coming as her "resurrection pose." Draw a picture of
your resurrection pose. Or write a poem describing the
resurrection of the body.

Thursday

READINGS: Ex 32:7–14 / Ps 106:19–20, 21–22, 23 / Jn 5:31–47

> "You search the scriptures, because you think you have eternal life through them; even they testify on my behalf. But you do not want to come to me to have life."
>
> —John 5:39–40

IN TODAY'S GOSPEL, JESUS basically says to the crowd, "You have studied the word of God and yet you do not recognize the incarnate Word of God standing before you." Jesus' words are particularly an indictment of the Pharisees and scribes, the religious "professionals" of his day who had dedicated their lives to knowing and living according to God's word. Today, some Christians interpret Jesus' many condemnations of the Pharisees and scribes to mean that he thought institutional religion was, at the very least, unnecessary. Others go further and insist Jesus taught that organized religion should be distrusted and is even poisonous. Nothing could be further from the truth.

Examples abound that demonstrate Jesus' strong ties with and respect for the practices of Judaism. He was born to righteous Jewish parents who followed the Law. His family went every year to the Temple in Jerusalem (see Lk 2:41–42). As an adult, he regularly traveled to the Jerusalem and attended synagogue. Jesus put on the tassels worn by all pious Jews at the time as a reminder to obey God's Law (see Mk 6:56). Jesus condemned the Pharisees and scribes not because they took the practice of their faith too seriously but because they only focused on certain aspects. Jesus thought that the Pharisees and scribes were merely partially wrong, and he deeply desired their full conversion. He tried to show them that religion cannot be merely exterior because humans are a union of body and soul. Faith, therefore, must be practiced both interiorly and exteriorly. When either is disregarded, it is impossible to know God to our fullest capacity.

Jesus' hard-hitting words are a challenge to both inner and outer conversion. One could imagine him saying to us, "You go through the motions, attend church, read the Bible, receive the sacraments, but you still do not recognize me?" Or, for those who fall prey to the opposite extreme, "You neglect to come to worship and to receive my graces regularly in the sacraments, and you think you know me?" In moments like this, Jesus insists, "Come to me" (Mt 11:28). Where is Jesus? He is in the Church: "He is the head of the body, the church" (Col

1:18). He is in the Eucharist: "I am the Bread of Life" (Jn 6:35). He is in the poor, the vulnerable, and the needy: "Whatever you did for one of these least brothers of mine, you did for me" (Mt 25:40). And through your Baptism, he is within each of us: "Whoever loves me will keep my word, and my Father will love him, and we will come to him and make our dwelling with him" (Jn 14:23).

As we remember our death daily, we also are reminded that the Lord longs for us to go to him, both exteriorly and interiorly, so that we may find life. In fact, we only remember death in order to remember Jesus who is life. Remembering that we might die helps us to savor each moment and to learn to search for the presence of Jesus. Death reminds us that our hope is in Jesus and that we should take advantage of all the ways we can go to Jesus while we still have the time.

Examen and Intercessory Prayer

Review your day (see the Memento Mori Daily Examen, p. 8).

Remember in your prayers those you know who feel distant from God. Pray a Hail Mary that all might come to experience interior and exterior conversion.

All the Savior's apparitions brought joy and consolation to souls. He appeared to Mary; and who can express with what a torrent of spiritual delight he inundated her heart? He appeared to Mary Magdalene, saying to her, "Mary" and this word alone, made him known. . . . He appeared to the Apostles, saying to them, "Peace be with you" and he said to them again. "Peace be with you" (Jn 20:19, 21). And the sight of him and these words filled all their hearts with joy: "The disciples rejoiced when they saw the Lord" (Jn 20:20). Let us learn to recognize by these signs the presence of Jesus Christ, and the characteristics that distinguish the action of his spirit in our souls from the action of the evil spirit. One announces himself by obscurity, trouble, depression, and agitation; the [Holy Spirit], on the contrary, announces himself by light, peace, interior consolation. Above all, let us know how to profit from the visits of Jesus Christ. . . . Consider with what loving tenderness, what effusion of heart, Jesus Christ deigns to console his Apostles—like a friend who, knowing the affliction of a friend tenderly loved, hastens to console him. [As you finish reading this] . . . say to yourself: If I am now raised to grace, I must, like Jesus Christ, make my resurrection shine for the glory of God and the edification of others. Jesus Christ risen dies no more; I must, then, die no more to grace by sin.

—Saint Ignatius of Loyola, *The Spiritual Exercises*

Journaling and Prayer

Reflect on the signs of the Holy Spirit's action that Saint Ignatius describes in the quote above. Identify some times in your life when you felt the action of the evil spirit and times when you felt the consolation of the Holy Spirit. Ask God for guidance.

Do you feel far from Jesus? Write down three ways that you can draw close to him in the coming week.

Friday

Readings: Wis 2:1a, 12–22 / Ps 34:17–18, 19–20, 21, 23 / Jn 7:1–2, 10, 25–30

Some of the inhabitants of Jerusalem said, "Is he not the one they are trying to kill? And look, he is speaking openly and they say nothing to him. Could the authorities have realized that he is the Messiah? But we know where he is from. When the Messiah comes, no one will know where he is from."

—John 7:25–27

THROUGHOUT THE GOSPELS, PEOPLE rejected Jesus because he seemed familiar to them, especially those who lived in the same city where he had grown up (see Mt 13:57, Mk 6:6). In today's Gospel, the people of Jerusalem rebuff the possibility that Jesus is the Messiah simply because they know his birth town. They cannot imagine that anyone important could come from a backwater town like Nazareth. The people's familiarity kills their curiosity and blinds them to the truth. Jesus must have suffered so much in the face of this bored familiarity that blocked the gift of faith—perhaps even more than when he faced outright hostility and violence.

If we don't want to be like the crowds in today's readings who completely fail to see Jesus, we must resist the false idea that familiarity is the same as banality. Jesus suffers when we pretend we know all there is to know about him. He also suffers when we reject him. We may insist that we would never reject Jesus and marvel that people did so while he was standing right before them. But we also sometimes respond to Jesus with similar prideful boredom and jaded familiarity. We reject Jesus when we can only see what irritates us at Mass rather than the glorious mystery, or when we reject someone who loves Christ because their idiosyncrasies annoy us. We turn our backs on Christ when we demonize and dehumanize other people made in the image of God, or when we ignore the poor and vulnerable right before us. If we are honest with ourselves, we reject Jesus all the time.

Perhaps we resist entering into the mystery of Jesus not only because we are prideful but also because we are trying to avoid death. To understand Jesus' true identity, beyond our tired assumptions and bored familiarity, we must be willing to contemplate and enter into Jesus' death. In fact, the Christian faith is centered on how Jesus' death has transformed our own. Thinking of death helps us to fully realize all that Jesus is and all that he has done for us. By remembering our death, we reject a superficial understanding of Jesus and enter into "the inscrutable riches of Christ" (Eph 3:8). However, if we choose to avoid death, we avoid Jesus.

Examen and Intercessory Prayer

Review your day (see the Memento Mori Daily Examen, p. 8).

Think of the people in your life who may believe but are lukewarm in their faith. Pray a Hail Mary for all lukewarm believers.

> Christ suffered in the friends who deserted him, and in his good name through the blasphemies hurled against him; in his honor and glory, from the mockeries and the insults heaped upon him. He suffered in things, for he was despoiled of his garments; in his soul, from sadness, weariness, and fear; in his body, from wounds and scourgings.
>
> . . . . Consider what he underwent in his various parts: his head suffered from the crown of piercing thorns, his hands and feet through the nails driven through them, his face from the blows and the defiling spittle, and his whole body through the lashes. He suffered in every sense of his body. Touch was afflicted by the scourging and the nailing, taste by the vinegar and gall he drank, smell by the stench of corpses as he hung on the Cross in that place of the dead called Calvary. His hearing was tormented with the cries of scorners and blasphemers, and in sight, by beholding the tears of his mother and of the disciple whom he loved. . . . The very least of Christ's sufferings was

sufficient in itself to redeem the human race from all its sins. But if we look at the fitness of the matter, it had to be that Christ should suffer in all the kinds of sufferings.

—Saint Thomas Aquinas, *Summa Theologiae, III.46.5*

Journaling and Prayer

Reflect on times when prideful familiarity has led you to irreverence toward God or neighbor.

Write a prayer to God asking to grow in wonder.

Saturday

READINGS: JER 11:18–20 / PS 7:2–3, 9BC–10, 11–12 / JN 7:40–53

A division occurred in the crowd because of him.

—John 7:43

IN TODAY'S GOSPEL, THE PEOPLE cannot decide on Jesus' true identity. Is he a prophet? Is he the Messiah? Is he a fake? The crowd is divided. Jesus disrupts—Truth always does. The author of the Letter to the Hebrews describes the incisive, challenging effect that Jesus' truth has on people: "the word of God is living and effective, sharper than any two-edged sword, penetrating even between soul and spirit, joints and marrow, and able to discern reflections and thoughts of the heart" (4:12). God's Word is Jesus, and his identity cuts right to the heart. The Word of God pierces souls and penetrates both our minds and our hearts.

However, like the people in the crowd, when we are met with the person of Jesus we are divided. This division occurs in two ways. First, it happens interiorly. We want to believe in the words of Jesus and to follow him to new life. But we are divided because we also want to forget his troubling demands for change. Second, when we begin to choose to follow Christ, we experience great division exteriorly. Prioritizing the Gospel concretely in our lives in a healthy but also a radical way can cause other people who love us to respond negatively. Some oppose us because they hate religion. Others resent moving to second place in our lives. Still others are frightened or bitter because our conversion of life calls them to similar changes.

Following Jesus requires death. In the midst of interior and exterior division, we must be willing to die to many of our desires and expectations. The people we thought would remain by our side might disappear. And those we expected to leave immediately might remain. The most religious people in our lives may, surprisingly, resent our radical discipleship more than the less religious. People will surprise us in good ways and bad. But in the midst of the confusion, we can remain by Christ's side, knowing that he will bring good from this dying to ourselves. As Saint Paul reminds us: "If, then, we have died with Christ, we believe that we shall also live with him" (Rom 6:8). Everything in our being may resist dying with Jesus. Nevertheless, we can ask Jesus to open our hearts to listen to his voice. In the power of Jesus Christ, we can walk with him through the screaming interior and exterior voices to the Place of the Skull. The Son of God will lead us through death to new life and to powerful unity of heart.

Examen and Intercessory Prayer

Review your day (see the Memento Mori Daily Examen, p. 8).

Think of someone you know who opposes your discipleship. Pray a Hail Mary for this person and for all who resist the call of Jesus in their own lives and in their loved ones' lives.

Seeing, then, that all things have an end, these two things are simultaneously set before us—death and life; and everyone will experience it. For as there are two kinds of coins, the one of God, the other of the world, and each has its special character stamped upon it [so is it also here.] The unbelieving are of this world; but the believing have, in love, the character of God the Father by Jesus Christ, by whom, if we are not ready to die into his passion, his life is not in us.

. . . I exhort you to learn to do all things with a divine harmony, while your bishop presides in the place of God, and your presbyters in the place of the assembly of the apostles, along with your deacons, who are most dear to me, and are entrusted with the ministry of Jesus Christ, who was with the Father before the beginning of time, and in the end was revealed. Do all then, imitating the same divine conduct, pay respect to one another . . . continually love each other in Jesus Christ. Let nothing exist among you that may divide you; but be united with your bishop, and those who preside over you, as a type and evidence of your immortality.

—Saint Ignatius of Antioch, *Epistle to the Magnesians*

Journaling and Prayer

Consider a time that you felt tempted to make a bad choice but through God's grace you chose the good. Give thanks to God and ask him how you can make more choices like this in the future.

Draw a symbol that represents the battle between life and death within your soul. Or write a prayer thanking Jesus for already winning the battle and ask him to help you to grow in trust.

Fifth Week of Lent

Saint Mary Magdalene, Giovanni Antonio Galli. The Walters Art Museum. Acquired by Henry Walters with the Massarenti Collection.

Sunday

Scrutiny Readings: Ez 37:12–14 / Ps 130:1–2, 3–4, 5–6, 7–8 / Rom 8:8–11 / Jn 11:1–45

> [Jesus] told them, "Our friend Lazarus is asleep, but I am going to awaken him." So the disciples said to him, "Master, if he is asleep, he will be saved."
>
> —John 11:11–12

IN TODAY'S GOSPEL, JESUS tells the disciples that he is going to awaken the sleeping Lazarus. The disciples know that Lazarus is ill and they also must be familiar with the use of sleep as a metaphor for death in the Scriptures. Yet, they choose to assume that Jesus is talking about ordinary sleep. Perhaps the disciples want to believe that Lazarus was just sleeping because death deeply terrifies them, as it terrifies most people. Understandably, the disciples want to believe in the most consoling possibility. Sleep is temporary—one can go to sleep for a time and awaken restored and refreshed, ready for another day. Death, on the other hand, is permanent, the end of earthly life. No second chances, no redos, no rewind.

However, whether Lazarus is asleep or dead, the disciples' relief that Jesus could take care of the situation is an entirely appropriate response. Jesus has power over life and death. To bring a pile of bones and dust to life is child's play for the Creator of the Universe. After all, God created the entire world from absolutely nothing. However, the disciples still do not fully understand who they are dealing with. When the Son of God arrives in Bethany, no one expects a miracle. Upon Jesus' arrival, though Martha declares that Jesus is the Messiah and the Son of God (see Jn 11:27), no one yet understands exactly what that means. When Jesus asks them to roll away the stone from Lazarus' tomb, Martha voices everyone's doubts. She points out that it will smell terrible because her brother's corpse has been rotting away for four days. But Jesus insists, knowing the Father's power. Jesus calls out and as his voice enters the darkness "the dead man came out" (Jn 11:44).

Lazarus' resurrection should absolutely astonish us. Jesus merely spoke Lazarus' name and his friend's corpse rose to life again. The power of the voice of Jesus! "He utters his voice and the earth melts" (Ps 46:7). However, Jesus' primary mission is even more astonishing. Jesus came not merely to bring life to dead bodies. He came to bring life to both bodies and souls deadened by sin. In order to do this, Jesus accepted death and overcame it with his divine life. The Cross awakens us from the slumber of our ignorance and sin and pours on us God's saving grace. Jesus can help us to "be vigilant at all times" (Lk 21:36) so that death may be but a momentary slumber until we awake forever in God's heavenly kingdom.

Examen and Intercessory Prayer

Review your day (see the Memento Mori Daily Examen, p. 8).

Think of the people you know who are terminally ill or face any kind of death sentence. Pray a Hail Mary for all those who know that they will die in the near future.

It is a childish terror to fear death but not to fear sin. Little children are afraid of masks, but do not fear the fire. Quite the opposite, if they are accidently carried too near a lighted candle, they stretch out their hand without any concern for the candle and the flame. Yet a mask . . . terrifies them while they have no dread of fire, which is really the thing they should fear. Just so, we too have a fear of death, which is a mask that might well be despised; but we have no fear of sin, which is truly dreadful. . . . And this is likely to happen not on account of the nature of the things, but because of our own foolishness. . . . What then, I pray you, is death? Just like putting off a garment. The body is about the soul as a garment; and after laying it aside for a short time by means of death, we will resume it again with even more splendor. What is death at most? It is a journey for a season; a sleep longer than usual! So that if you fear death, you should also fear sleep! . . . Sorrow not for the dying person; but sorrow for those who are living in sin!

—Saint John Chrysostom, *Homily 5 on the Statues*

Journaling and Prayer

Imagine you are Lazarus in the tomb surrounded by the smell of death and the bones of your favorite sins. Hear Jesus' voice calling out to you. How do you respond? Do you want to leave or are you afraid? Take some time to sit with this scene in your imagination and write down what Jesus says to you and what you experience.

Write a prayer to Jesus asking him to raise you from the death of your sins.

Monday

READINGS: DN 13:1–9, 15–17, 19–30, 33–62 / PS 23:1–3A, 3B–4, 5, 6 / JN 8:1–11

> "Neither do I condemn you. Go, and from now on do not sin any more."
>
> —John 8:11

IN TODAY'S GOSPEL, A crowd gathers around Jesus early in the morning. A woman caught in the act of adultery—a sin necessarily involving two people—is brought alone before Jesus. She stands ashamed and afraid in the middle of the crowd. The scribes and the Pharisees are eager to punish the sins of the woman, but they are even more eager to entrap Jesus. They want to see if Jesus will follow the Law of Moses and condemn her to death. And Jesus responds exactly as they have come to expect—unexpectedly. Crouching down, he traces something in the dirt. Some have theorized that Jesus was writing the sins of the people standing in front of him in the dust. Whether this is true or not, Jesus saw the hearts of the people around him that day. He then said, "Let the one among you who is without sin be the first to throw a stone at her" (Jn 8:7).

As he often does, Jesus showed the crowd an uncomfortable truth that day. Sin is not "out there" in the person or group one judges to be most sinful—it is in all human hearts. Everyone is a sinner who needs redemption. Every single person standing before Jesus that day was under a death sentence for their sin, not just the adulterous woman. Thankfully, Jesus judges just as he acts—unexpectedly. Neither the scribes nor the Pharisees realize it, but Jesus has more authority than a mere judge. He is not simply an arbitrator of the law. Rather, Jesus himself is the New Law. When he chooses not to condemn the woman, Jesus demonstrates that he is greater than the Law of Moses. He does not minimize or make light of the woman's sins, but he measures them against himself.

That day, Jesus lifted the adulterous woman's condemnation through the power of his life, death, and resurrection. And, if they were to accept it, he also would lift the condemnation of every person in the crowd. Jesus showed himself to be not only that woman's Savior on that particular day but also the Savior of every person in the crowd—and the Savior of every person who would ever live. Death without a Savior is a tragedy, an end, a horrible finality. With Jesus Christ, death becomes an invitation to a beautiful eternity with the one who made us. When we remember death we also remember Jesus, our Merciful Judge, who has wiped our death sentence away.

Examen and Intercessory Prayer

Review your day (see the Memento Mori Daily Examen, p. 8).

Think of a person or group that you tend to judge as more sinful than you. Pray a Hail Mary that all sinners might turn to Jesus, including yourself.

Were you bad yesterday? Today be good. Have you continued in your wickedness today? At any rate, change tomorrow. You are always waiting and you promise yourself a lot from the mercy of God. As if he, who promised you pardon through repentance, has also promised you a longer life. How do you know what tomorrow might bring? Rightly you say in your heart: "When I have corrected my ways, God will put all my sins away." We cannot deny that God has promised pardon to those who have amended their ways and are converted. [But] where has God also promised a long life to the one who makes amends? . . . The one who says, "God is good, God is merciful, let me do whatever I please, whatever I like. Let me loosen the reins of my lusts; let me gratify the cravings of my soul." Why? Because God is merciful, God is good, God is kind? These people endanger themselves by hope. And others who fall into grievous sins and think that they cannot be pardoned upon repentance endanger themselves by their despair. . . . Accordingly, for the sake of those who endanger themselves by despair, [God] has offered us a refuge of pardon. And for those who endanger themselves by hope, and are deluded by delays, he has made the day of death uncertain. You know not when your last day may come. Are you ungrateful because you have today on which you can improve? As he said to the [adulterous] woman, "Neither will I condemn you. But, now that you are secure concerning the past, beware of the future. Neither will I condemn you: I have blotted out what you have done; now keep what I have commanded you, so that you might find what I have promised."

—Saint Augustine, *Tractate 33*
on the Gospel of John

Journaling and Prayer

Remember a sin that you may have confessed but still haunts your memory. Stand before Jesus and imagine a jeering crowd behind you. As tears fall down your face, ask Jesus how he is going to judge you. Remain in prayer for some time and then write down what you experience.

Draw something based on what you heard in prayer or write any words you heard from Jesus in your heart.

Tuesday

READINGS: Nm 21:4–9 / Ps 102:2–3, 16–18, 19–21 / Jn 8:21–30

> "I am going away and you will look for me, but you will die in your sin. Where I am going you cannot come."
>
> —John 8:21

THE WORDS IN TODAY'S Gospel are terrifying. Over and over, Jesus had revealed his divine identity and still many people did not understand. Ever-patient, Jesus tries to tell them clearly and bluntly the consequences of their rejection. He understands the human tendency to put things off, to think that there will be plenty of time to figure things out later. So Jesus warns the people that he will not be around forever to explain the mysteries of heaven.

Jesus continues to explain to the crowd that he will soon be lifted up on the Cross, as Moses lifted up the serpent in the desert (see Jn 8:28). The crowd would have been familiar with Jesus' reference. When the Israelites were dying in the desert from the bite of poisonous serpents, God had told Moses to make a bronze serpent and to lift it up. God promised that everyone who had been bitten could "look at it and recover" (Nm 21:8). Jesus is clearly making a similar promise. But this time, rather than a serpent, Jesus' bloodied body will be raised as the new source of healing. Even if the people did not completely understand Jesus' words, this must have been a shocking image for them to ponder. Upon hearing Jesus describe this scene, "many came to believe in him" (Jn 8:30).

You will die in your sin. Today, some people continue to ignore Jesus' warning. They refuse to gaze in faith at Jesus on the Cross. Instead, they see Jesus' bloodied body and turn away either in disbelief or disgust. They assume a poor carpenter's spilled blood cannot heal their broken hearts, cannot give them what they most deeply desire. But they are wrong. Jesus' bloodied body does heal. Sometimes when we remember death we also should gaze on the crucifix. As the people gazed on the serpent in the desert and were healed, Jesus wants us to gaze upon the crucifix and be healed. Jesus wants us to look at him and to let him look at us. We can find healing by gazing at the God who loved us so much that he was lifted up on the wood of the Cross like a common criminal. If we stand beneath the Cross and let the Son of God's blood fall on us and roll into our hearts, we can be sure that we will not die in our sin.

Examen and Intercessory Prayer

Review your day (see the Memento Mori Daily Examen, p. 8).

Think of the people in your life who turn their face away from Jesus and who do not believe in God. Pray a Hail Mary for all unbelievers.

> This Blood causes the image of our King to be fresh within us, produces unspeakable beauty, prevents the nobleness of our souls from wasting away, watering it continually, and nourishing it. The Blood derived from [the Eucharist] . . . waters our souls, and works in them a mighty power. This Blood, if rightly taken, drives away demons and keeps them far off from us, while it calls to us angels. . . . Wherever they see the Lord's Blood, devils flee, and angels run together. This Blood poured forth washed clean the entire world. . . . This Blood is the salvation of our souls, by this the soul is washed, by this it is beautiful, by this it is inflamed. It causes our understanding to be brighter than fire and our soul to beam more than gold; this Blood was poured forth and made heaven accessible. . . . This Blood was ever typified of old in the altars and sacrifices of righteous men, the price of the world. By it Christ purchased for himself the Church, by it he has adorned her. . . . Christ has purchased us with his Blood, and adorned us with his Blood. Those who share this Blood stand with angels and archangels and the powers of heaven, clothed in Christ's own kingly robe and with the armor of the Spirit. Nay, I have not as yet said any great thing: they are clothed with the King himself.
>
> —Saint John Chrysostom, *Homily 46
> on the Gospel of John*

Journaling and Prayer

Imagine yourself beneath the Cross. Look up at Jesus. Do not turn away from his bloodied face. Gaze at him and allow his wounds to heal you. Take time to remain in prayer, and then write down what you experience.

Draw an image related to the blood of Christ. Or write a prayer of thanksgiving for the blood of Jesus Christ.

Wednesday

READINGS: DN 3:14–20, 91–92, 95 / DN 3:52, 53, 54, 55, 56 / JN 8:31–42

"If you remain in my word, you will truly be my disciples, and you will know the truth, and the truth will set you free."

—John 8:31–32

IN TODAY'S GOSPEL, JESUS assures the people that if they believe in him and remain in his word, they will know the truth. However, the people angrily reject the idea that Jesus is a source of truth. People often reject Jesus in this way. They believe in the existence of truth but they do not accept that Jesus is the Truth that will set them free. Others reject Jesus with a different kind of skepticism. They are like Pontius Pilate who asked Jesus on Good Friday, "What is truth?" (Jn 18:38). For them, truth either does not exist or is unknowable. If Jesus truly is God who is Truth itself, then neither of these positions is tenable.

As Christians, we base our belief in Jesus Truth not only on faith but on reason and historical evidence. Both Scripture and other ancient sources acknowledge the empty tomb. The Apostles' overnight change from cowards to bold witnesses after Jesus' resurrection also supports the reality of the resurrection. The Apostles were suddenly willing to die for Jesus because they had seen him resurrected. Reasons to believe that the resurrection is an historical fact abound, and if one accepts the historical fact of the resurrection, then one must accept that Jesus is God. After all, only the Creator of Life could have brought himself back to life. And the reality of God is such that he is not merely a being among beings—another object in the universe—or even a mere transmitter of truth. Rather, God is the cause of all that exists. There is no other source of truth that can be found but in God. Jesus *is* the living Truth (see Jn 14:6). Therefore, to reject Jesus' truth is to reject not just what he says, but to reject Truth itself.

Jesus' encouragement to remain in his truth in today's Gospel also applies to our remembrance of death. Physical death is a hard and difficult truth. But we face it knowing it is not the entire truth. Jesus is the entire reality of Truth, the source of truth. God's very existence and nature is the truth that will set us free. We find truth when we accept not only that we will die but also when we accept God who is Truth. Every time we reject Jesus and stray from his truth, we also reject God who has caused our existence. We reject our identity that can only be found in our Creator. Our life, our identity, and our truth are found only in God. When we remember death, we plunge our future into this dazzling Truth that gives us life.

Examen and Intercessory Prayer

Review your day (see the Memento Mori Daily Examen, p. 8).

Think of those you know who genuinely search for truth. Pray a Hail Mary for all truth seekers, including yourself, that they might always find truth in God.

> On a certain day, I took up a pearl, my brethren; I saw in it mysteries pertaining to the Kingdom; semblances and types of the Majesty; it became a fountain, and I drank out of it the mysteries of the Son.
>
> I put it, my brethren, on the palm of my hand, that I might examine it: I looked at it from one side, and it had faces on all sides. I found out that the Son was incomprehensible, since he is wholly Light.
>
> In its brightness I beheld the Bright One who cannot be clouded, and in its pureness a great mystery, even the Body of our Lord which is well-refined: in its undividedness I saw the Truth which is undivided.
>
> I saw therein its pure conception—the Church, and the Son within her. The cloud was the likeness of her who bore him, and her type the heavens, since there shone forth from her his gracious Shining.
>
> —Saint Ephrem the Syrian, *The Pearl*

Journaling and Prayer

Reflect on your desire to be free. What does freedom mean to you? Take some time to pray with Jesus and consider whether you refer to his truth when you make choices.

Draw the pearl that Saint Ephrem speaks about in the reflection. Or write a prayer to Jesus Truth asking him to set you free.

Thursday

READINGS: GN 17:3–9 / PS 105:4–5, 6–7, 8–9 / JN 8:51–59

"Whoever keeps my word will never see death."

—John 8:51

THE GOOD NEWS IS met with disbelief and violence throughout Scripture—even from Jesus' closest friends. In fact, Jesus probably did not broadcast the exact nature of his mission for a long time because he knew it would not be received well. Instead, he slowly revealed his true identity—first to his Apostles and, finally, by preaching to the crowds. In today's Gospel, Jesus plainly reveals his identity to the crowds. But first, he tells them his mission—to save them from death. Their reaction makes clear why Jesus waited so long to reveal this good news. Instead of rejoicing, the people angrily suggest that Jesus is possessed by the devil (see Jn 8:52).

Unperturbed by the people's lack of understanding, Jesus continues. He reveals something even more scandalous, saying, "Amen, amen, I say to you, before Abraham came to be, I AM" (Jn 8:58). "I AM" would have been both an unmistakable and a shocking phrase for the people listening. Jesus identifies himself with the same words God used when Moses asked for his name (see Ex 3:14). When the people hear Jesus' claim to divinity, they are filled with anger and pick up stones to kill him (see Jn 8:59). The idea that God would be-come a man was not just absurd to the crowd but downright blasphemous. However, at this point in Jesus' mission, he wants to reveal everything. He has revealed that his purpose in coming to earth is to save everyone from death. And now Jesus makes clear how he can take on this awe-inspiring task—because he is God. Who else would have the power to defeat death?

When we remember our death, we also should remember that Jesus has saved us from it. This two-fold meditation should never be unwound as it defeats the purpose of *memento mori*. When we forget or refuse to accept that Jesus came to save us from death, we are like the people in today's Gospel. We hear what Jesus has to say and then we pick up stones to bash him in the head. We want to kill the messenger because he demands something from us. We prefer to drive our Savior from our hearts with the stones of sin rather than allow him to save us from death. But Jesus' grace is always more powerful than the stones of sin that we grip. His grace smashes the rocks in our hands and the stony exterior of our hearts and helps us to accept the Good News. This news is stunning, challenging, and difficult to accept—but ultimately, if we accept it, it will lead us to Life itself.

Examen and Intercessory Prayer

Review your day (see the Memento Mori Daily Examen, p. 8).

Think of the people in countries where it is dangerous to be Christian. Pray a Hail Mary for all who are persecuted for practicing their faith.

> Death's name is terrible. Usually when it is spoken, someone says: "Your dear father is dead," or "your son is dead." This is not well said among Christians. We should say, "Your son or your father has gone to his country and to yours; and because necessity required it, he passed by the way of death, in which he lingered not." I certainly do not know how we can regard as our country this world, in which we remain for so short a time, compared with heaven, in which we shall dwell forever. Let us go forward then, and be more assured of the presence of our dear friends who are above, than of those who are here below. . . . And if the departure of a sweet soul causes the remains of sadness to still weigh down your mind, then cast yourself on your knees before the heart of our crucified Savior and ask his assistance. He will give it to you and will inspire you with the thought and the resolution to prepare yourself well to make the same passage when it is your turn, and at the appointed hour when you may happily arrive at the place where we should hope our poor but blessed deceased are now safely lodged.
>
> —Saint Francis de Sales

Journaling and Prayer

Imagine you are in the crowd when Jesus reveals that he is God. Try to put yourself there, feel what they felt, and seek to understand how they were challenged. Ask God to help you to see how similar reactions play out in your life.

Draw a picture of a stone—representing the sin you struggle with most—being smashed by the power of God's grace.

Friday

READINGS: JER 20:10–13 / PS 18:2–3A, 3BC–4, 5–6, 7 / JN 10:31–42

The cords of death encompassed me;
    the torrents of destruction terrified me.
The cords of Sheol encircled me;
    the snares of death lay in wait for me.
In my distress I called out: LORD!
    I cried out to my God.
From his temple he heard my voice;
    my cry to him reached his ears.

—Psalm 18:5–7

SINCE ANCIENT TIMES, THE span of one's life has been poetically compared to a piece of thread that death eventually severs. In Greek mythology, three goddesses called the *Moirai* or "Fates" were each in charge of a different aspect of a person's thread. One spun the thread of life, another measured its length, and another cut it. The Hebrew Scriptures also use the thread metaphor for life's length. In today's readings, for example, the thread of life takes on a threatening form. For the psalmist, the thread of life is like the "cords of death" that curl round and round him until he chokes out his last breath. All of life is framed by this sorrowful end.

For humanity, death is truly an inescapable snare. The psalmist accurately describes the state of human existence: trapped like hunters' prey by an inevitable, baffling conclusion. Voicing humanity's desperation in the face of this reality, the psalmist cries out in despair, "Lord!" In the Book of Isaiah, King Hezekiah expresses to God a similar desperation as he faces death: "You have folded up my life, like a weaver who severs me from the last thread" (38:12). God hears Hezekiah's cry and adds fifteen years to his life, but the king knows that eventually mortality will catch up with him and the thread of his life will be severed.

When we remember our death, we choose to enter into the desperate cry that both the psalmist and King Hezekiah express. If we refuse to enter this cry, then life takes on a frenetic pace as we run from the inevitable. Skimming the surface, we flee from reality. All the while, deep down we know that we can really never escape the end that lurks beneath the trajectory of our lives. Though difficult, we must allow our awareness of death to surround us like cords until we are pulled under. Only then will we truly understand the stunning nature of the incarnation and the passion, death, and resurrection of Jesus Christ. Though it can be frightening and stressful at times, we remember death knowing that Jesus will hear our voice and reach below the raging waters to pull us out. We have only to wait upon his saving hand. Our cry will reach his ears. And when it does, we will sing the words that King Hezekiah prophesied in hope:

> The LORD is there to save us.
>> We shall play our music
> In the house of the LORD
>> all the days of our life (Is 38:20).

Examen and Intercessory Prayer

Review your day (see the Memento Mori Daily Examen, p. 8).

Think of anyone you know who is expecting a child. Pray a Hail Mary for all expecting mothers and fathers.

[The Lord speaking to Saint Catherine of Genoa]: [My] love transforms beasts into humans, humans into angels, and angels become like God, by participation. People change from being earthly to heavenly, devoting themselves in both soul and body to the practice of spiritual things. Their whole life and way of speaking are altered, and they do and say the contrary of what they used to do. All are surprised at this. . . . No one comprehends how this happens unless they have experienced it themselves. That deep, sweet, and penetrating love that one feels in the heart is mysterious, and cannot be described or understood. . . . Remaining quiet and satisfied in the inmost heart, one knows this love and knows it alone. Kept closely bound by a very subtle thread held secretly by my hand, the person is allowed to struggle and combat with the world, the devil, and himself. Fainting, weak, and helpless, the person fears ruin on every side but I do not allow him to fall. . . . I let down into the person's heart a slender, golden thread of my hidden love. Attached to the thread is a hook that enters the heart, and one feels wounded, but knows not by whom he is bound and taken. The person neither moves nor wishes to move, because the heart is drawn by me, its object and its end, although he does not comprehend it. But it is I who hold the thread in my hand, and draw it even closer with such a penetrating and subtle love.

—Saint Catherine of Genoa, *Spiritual Dialogues*

Journaling and Prayer

The Psalms capture life's emotional highs and lows and show us that God always wants to hear exactly what is on our hearts. Read Psalm 18 slowly and choose the line that you most identify with right now. Spend some time in prayer sharing your troubles and joys, and listen to God's response.

Draw the thread of your life and its connection with God. Or write a prayer asking Jesus to save you from the cords of death.

Saturday

READINGS: EZ 37:21–28 / JER 31:10, 11–13 / JN 11:45–56

> "The Romans will come and take away both our land and our nation."
>
> —John 11:48

JESUS' RADICAL TEACHING WERE so unsettling that, in today's readings, the religious establishment gathers to discuss permanent solutions. The Sanhedrin had legitimate concerns that many Christians voice today—to protect both "land" and "nation." The unrest Jesus had caused was heading toward a Roman crackdown with the potential to destroy the vulnerable Jewish community. The men of the Sanhedrin had dedicated everything to God and were concerned for the lives of their families, young children, and the future of their religion. Understandably, they preferred the status quo to the possibility of losing everything. But what may have begun as legitimate concerns for both "land" and "nation," soon grew into priorities that superseded God's will. The Sanhedrin's compelling concerns ended up drowning out God's voice.

We often respond to God's call similarly when we put other concerns before God and the goal of eternal life. Jesus' call to follow him requires us to step away from comfort and predictability and to be willing to leave behind everything if necessary—even those things that are rightfully important to us. We are called to radically strip away all of the -isms that keep us from totally giving our lives to Jesus: materialism, nationalism, consumerism, individualism, relativism, etc. In short, God calls us to tear down our idols. When we refuse to smash our idols, we turn religion into something other than following Jesus. We crucify Jesus in our hearts.

Of course, sometimes our idols are legitimate concerns. In fact, these are often the most convincing idols because they are rightfully important. Love of country, love of family, love of aspects of the faith are all important. However, when Jesus calls us to follow him to the Place of the Skull, he invites us to leave behind even those things we legitimately and passionately love. Thus, he says, "Do you think that I have come to establish peace on the earth? No, I tell you, but rather division" (Lk 12:51). Following Jesus is all or nothing. Family cannot come first. Country cannot come first. Even aspects of the faith cannot come first. Jesus must come first. Every time Christ asks us to follow him and to rip ourselves away from the things we love, we enter more deeply into Christ's death that brings new life.

Examen and Intercessory Prayer

Review your day (see the Memento Mori Daily Examen, p. 8).

Bring to mind all of the catechumens in your parish, or someone you know who is considering the faith. Pray a Hail Mary for all catechumens that they will be protected from spiritual attacks as they leave everything behind to follow Jesus.

Following God's way leads to life, whereas following idols leads to death. . . . God is the Living One, the Merciful One; Jesus brings us the life of God; the Holy Spirit gives and keeps us in our new life as true sons and daughters of God. But all too often, as we know from experience, people do not choose life, they do not accept the "Gospel of Life" but let themselves be led by ideologies and ways of thinking that block life, that do not respect life, because they are dictated by selfishness, self-interest, profit, power, and pleasure, and not by love, by concern for the good of others. It is the eternal dream of wanting to build the city of man without God, without God's life and love—a new Tower of Babel. It is the idea that rejecting God, the message of Christ, the Gospel of Life, will somehow lead to freedom, to complete human fulfillment. As a result, the Living God is replaced by fleeting human idols that offer the intoxication of a flash of freedom, but in the end bring new forms of slavery and death. The wisdom of the psalmist says: "The precepts of the LORD are right, rejoicing the heart; the commandment of the LORD is pure, enlightening the eyes" (Ps 19:8). Let us always remember: the Lord is the Living One, he is merciful. Dear brothers and sisters, let us look to God as the God of Life, let us look to his law, to the Gospel message, as the way to freedom and life. The Living God sets us free! Let us say "Yes" to love and not to selfishness. Let us say "Yes" to life and not to death. Let us say "Yes" to freedom and not to enslavement to the many idols of our time.

—Pope Francis, Homily for *Evangelium Vitae* Day

Journaling and Prayer

How often do valid concerns keep you from taking risks to follow Jesus and to spread the kingdom of God? What are the idols in your life? Take some time to pray with these questions, asking Jesus what loves, even legitimate ones, he is asking you to leave behind to follow him.

Draw something to represent the idols in your life being overcome by Christ. Or choose a line from the reflection that moves you and letter it in your journal.

Holy Week

Crucifixion with Saints, Fra Angelico.

Palm Sunday

READINGS: IS 50:4–7 / Ps 22:8–9, 17–18, 19–20, 23–24 / PHIL 2:6–11

GOSPEL YEAR A: MT 26:14 – 27:66; *YEAR B:* MK 14:1–15:47;
    YEAR C: LK 22:14 – 23:56

Peter followed him at a distance.

—Mark 14:54

ALL OF THE SYNOPTIC Gospels mention a small, easily overlooked detail in the Passion narratives. Peter follows Jesus to the high priest's courtyard "at a distance" (see Lk 22:54, Mt 26:58). Such a short phrase—but enough to communicate the flood of fear and sorrow that suddenly surged in Peter's heart on that fateful night. Only hours before, Peter had boldly promised Jesus, "Lord, I am prepared to go to prison and to die with you" (Lk 22:33). But, now, when faced with the real possibility of death rather than mere hypotheticals, Peter cowers in fear. In place of the honors and victory he had anticipated, Peter now realizes that his association with Jesus truly will put him in danger of death.

Fearful for his life, Peter puts distance between himself and the Lord. The Rock upon which Jesus intended to build his Church (see Mt 16:18) is afraid to walk closely with Jesus. The human tendency to pusillanimous, weak, and self-centered behavior is exemplified in Peter and the other disciples on the night Jesus is arrested. The Apostles, some of Jesus' closest friends, fall asleep as Jesus faces his darkest hour (see Mt 26:40). Then Jesus' followers run away when he is arrested (see Mk 14:15). Peter is a coward like the rest, but at least he follows Jesus at a distance. Jesus must have seen and appreciated this small sign of Peter's love, even if it was but a weak flicker.

By the end of his life, Peter followed Christ so closely that tradition relates he asked to be crucified upside down because he felt he did not deserve to die in the same manner as Jesus did. Peter's example can give us hope when we observe how faintly our love for God flickers in our hearts at times. Jesus sees our gutless, self-absorption and he still loves and reaches out to us. Jesus observes us following him "at a distance," and he nevertheless continues to fill our faint-hearted souls with grace. Our God of Life has mercy on us even in our most humiliating, cowardly moments because he knows what his grace can do in our lives. Peter's development in the spiritual life gives us confidence that, even in the midst of our failings, God will bless the little we do and helps us to grow in bold holiness. Like Peter, we can trust that death will become a privilege for those who, in God's grace, bravely continue to strive to follow Jesus.

Examen and Intercessory Prayer

Review your day (see the Memento Mori Daily Examen, p. 8).

Pray a Hail Mary for all those who struggle to follow God's plan when it requires great sacrifice.

O Lord, you have freed us from the fear of death. You have made the end of this life the beginning of true life. You rest our bodies in sleep for a season and awaken them again at the last trumpet. . . . One day you will take again what you have given, transfiguring our mortal and unsightly remains with immortality and grace. You have saved us from the curse and from sin, having become both for our sake. You have broken the head of the dragon that had seized us with his jaws, in the yawning gulf of disobedience. You have shown us the way of resurrection, broken the gates of hell, and brought to nothing the one who had the power of death—the devil. In the symbol of the Holy Cross, you have given a sign to those who fear you that destroys the adversary and saves our lives. O God eternal, to you I have been attached from my mother's womb, you whom my soul has loved with all its strength, to whom I have dedicated both my flesh and my soul from my youth up until now—give me an angel of light to conduct me to the place of refreshment, to the water of rest, in the bosom of the holy fathers. You who broke the flaming sword and restored to paradise the man who was crucified next to you and implored your mercies, remember me, too, in your kingdom. . . . O you who have power on earth to forgive sins, forgive me, that I may be refreshed when I put off my body and may be found before you without defilement on my soul. May my soul be received into your hands, spotless and undefiled, as an offering before you.

—Saint Macrina's dying prayer as recounted
by her brother, Saint Gregory of Nyssa

Journaling and Prayer

Imagine yourself in the scene as Peter follows Jesus to the high priest's house. Take some time to pray with Peter's feelings and conflicting desires to save himself and to follow Jesus. Ask God to shed light on how this plays out in your own life.

Write a prayer asking God for the grace to follow Jesus closely.

Monday

READINGS: IS 42:1–7 / PS 27:1, 2, 3, 13–14 / JN 12:1–11

Mary took a liter of costly perfumed oil made from genuine aromatic nard and anointed the feet of Jesus and dried them with her hair; the house was filled with the fragrance of the oil.

—John 12:3

THE ANOINTING AT BETHANY in today's readings is recounted in various ways in the Gospels. This is perhaps not only due to differing eyewitness accounts but also to the spiritual richness of an event that defied straightforward retelling. As Jesus says in the Gospel of Matthew after Mary anointed him, "Amen, I say to you, wherever this gospel is proclaimed in the whole world, what she has done will be spoken of, in memory of her" (26:13). Thus, the power of this intimate moment permeates all of history with its sweet perfume.

The anointing at Bethany is set against the context of many other momentous anointings in salvation history. Throughout Scripture, priests, prophets, and kings are anointed. Moses anoints his brother Aaron and his sons as priests (see Ex 28:41). In the city of Bethlehem, the prophet Samuel anoints David king of Israel (see 1 Sam 16:13). God commands Elijah to anoint Elisha as prophet and his successor (see 1 Kings 19:16). And in today's Gospel, the prophetess Mary anoints Jesus as a sign that he is the Christ, the Anointed One. But this anointing is different. Just as Jesus did not need to be baptized by John the Baptist, Jesus also does not need to be anointed by a prophet. He is already anointed with the Holy Spirit. Nevertheless, Jesus accepts Mary's anointing because it is a sign that he is not only the hoped for Messiah, the one anointed by the Lord, but he *is* the Lord. Mary does not anoint an ordinary, mortal priest, prophet, or king who will die, be buried in a tomb, and honored. Rather, Mary anoints the Prophet of all prophets, the King of all kings, the Great High Priest of all priests.

Mary's act of anointing testifies to Jesus' divinity and also foreshadows his resurrection. When Judas the Iscariot criticizes Mary for extravagantly wasting costly oil (see Jn 12:5), Jesus defends her by arguing that the anointing is for his burial. However, Jesus in his divinity already knew that his dead body would never be anointed and that this anointing would be seen as a sign of his incorruptibility in retrospect. Unlike all previous priests, prophets, and kings, the Son of God was only anointed in life, not in death. Jesus would rise to new life before the women could get to the tomb to anoint his body. Thus, Mary only anoints a living body instead of a dead one—the Living Body of Christ that in falling prey to death would thereby conquer it.

We too are anointed with the Holy Spirit in our Baptism. Through the power of the Cross, physical death, the separation of our bodies and souls, is merely temporary. Every day we can call to mind the last moment of our lives, that moment when we will take our last breath. As we do, we should also remember that Jesus has power over that moment. We will not disappear into oblivion. Rather, anointed by the sweet unction of the Holy Spirit, we can be confident that death will not be the last page in our story.

Examen and Intercessory Prayer

Review your day (see the Memento Mori Daily Examen, p. 8).

Bring to mind your parish priest(s), your local bishop, the pope, and all lay and religious leaders in your area. Pray a Hail Mary that all Church leaders will experience an evermore-profound anointing in the Spirit of the Lord.

> Whoever wishes to be truly faithful, anoint the feet of the Lord with precious ointment like Mary. . . . Anoint the feet of Jesus: follow in the Lord's footsteps by a good life. Wipe his feet with your hair. What you have in surplus (as the hair seems superfluous to the body), give to the poor, and you have wiped the feet of the Lord. You have something to spare of your abundance? It is superfluous to you, but necessary for the

feet of the Lord. . . . Those who live wickedly and bear the name of Christians, do injury to Christ. Of them it is said, that through them the name of the Lord is blasphemed [see Rom 2:24]. If through such people God's name is blasphemed, then through those who are good the name of the Lord is honored. Listen to the Apostle, when he says, "We are the aroma of Christ" [2 Cor 2:15]. As it is said also in the Song of Songs, "Your name is as ointment poured forth" [1:3] . . . That sweet odor is to some the savor of life unto life, and to others the odor of death unto death; and yet all the while it is a sweet odor in itself. . . . Happy are those who find life in this sweet savor! But what misery can be greater than theirs, to whom the sweet savor is the messenger of death?

—Saint Augustine, *Tractate 50 on the Gospel of John*

Journaling and Prayer

Picture yourself as Mary anointing the feet of Jesus. Remain in the scene and imagine what Jesus says to you. Take time to write down what you experience in prayer.

Write a list of the things in your life with which you anoint Jesus. What are the sweet odors of praise that you pour out on the King of the Universe?

Tuesday

READINGS: Is 49:1–6 / Ps 71:1–2, 3–4, 5–6, 15 AND 17 / Jn 13:21–33, 36–38

Peter said to him, "Master, why can't I follow you now? I will lay down my life for you." Jesus answered, "Will you lay down your life for me? Amen, amen, I say to you, the cock will not crow before you deny me three times."

—John 13:37–38

PETER'S EXCHANGE WITH JESUS in today's Gospel is heartbreaking in light of the fact that he would deny Jesus that very night. In this context, Peter's bravado sounds almost pathetic. All of his characteristic boldness would disappear in the face of death. Frightened for his life, the strong words he had said hours before—"I will lay down my life for you"—shatter in an instant, replaced with sheer existential terror. Peter's denial of Jesus is firmly rooted in an intense fear of death; a fear that the devil surely encouraged. His denial shows us

189

how fear of death can lead us so easily away from God's peace and into sin.

Of course, some fear of death is normal and not necessarily bad. Blessed James Alberione once wrote, "Death is repugnant to nature; thus nature rebels at the thought of it. We should not be surprised at this. Our Divine Savior himself, who became like us in all but sin, felt this repugnance also." We can be comforted by the fact that, in the face of death, Jesus too was overwhelmed with fear and sorrow. In the Garden of Gethsemane, he says, "My Father, if it is possible, let this cup pass from me" (Mt 26:39). However, Jesus' fear differs from Peter's in a fundamental way. Jesus expresses fear, but he concludes with an act of trust in the Father by saying, "Yet, not as I will, but as you will" (26:39).

Jesus models for us what we should do when we feel overcome by a fear of death. Peter's example after the resurrection shows us that a stance of trust is possible. Although he could not bring himself to demonstrate this kind of trust before Jesus' death, everything changed at Pentecost. That day in the Upper Room, the same Apostles who were overcome by a fear of death on the night of Jesus' crucifixion received the gift of the Spirit. The flame of God's love enabled many of them, including Peter, to face terrible martyrdom with courage. When we are overcome by a paralyzing fear of death, we can remember that we too have the gift of the Spirit. This Spirit empowers us to face death with trust, just as Jesus did. And while our fear of death may never be completely erased in this life, the Holy Spirit fills us with a daring courage that we never could have summoned on our own. Immersed in the power of the Holy Spirit, we can refuse to deny Jesus and reject all of the devil's deadly temptations.

Examen and Intercessory Prayer

Review your day (see the Memento Mori Daily Examen, p. 8).

Bring to mind anyone you know who struggles with excessive worry and stress. Pray a Hail Mary for those who suffer from anxiety.

> Later on, when the way of perfection was opened out before me, I realized that in order to become a saint one must suffer much, always seek the most perfect path, and forget oneself. I also understood that there are many degrees of holiness, and that each soul is free to respond to the calls of Our Lord, to do a great deal or little for his love—in a word, to choose among the sacrifices he asks. And then also, as in the days of my childhood, I cried out: "My God, I choose everything, I will not be a saint by halves, I am not afraid of suffering for you, I only fear one thing, and that is to do my own will. Accept the offering of my will, for I choose all that you will." . . . I remember a dream I [had as a child] which impressed itself very deeply on my memory. I thought I was walking alone in the garden when, suddenly, I saw near the arbor two hideous little devils dancing with surprising agility on a barrel of lime, despite the heavy irons attached to their feet. At first they cast fiery glances at me. Then, as though suddenly terrified, I saw them, in the twinkling of an eye, throw themselves down to the bottom of the barrel,

from which they came out somehow, only to run and hide themselves in the laundry that opened into the garden. Finding them such cowards, I wanted to know what they were going to do, and, overcoming my fears, I went to the window. The wretched little creatures were there, running about on the tables, not knowing how to hide themselves from my gaze. From time to time they came nearer, peering through the windows with an uneasy air, then, seeing that I was still there, they began to run about again looking quite desperate. Of course this dream was nothing extraordinary. Yet I think Our Lord made use of it to show me that a soul in the state of grace has nothing to fear from the devil, who is a coward, and will fly even from a little child's gaze.

—Saint Thérèse of Lisieux, *Story of a Soul*

Journaling and Prayer

Read today's Gospel and imagine yourself in the scene of the Last Supper. Which Apostle are you? How do you feel when Jesus says that someone will betray him? Stay in the scene and draw nearer to Jesus. Talk to him and listen to his response.

Draw something or someone from the scene of the Last Supper that moves you. Or hand letter a short phrase from the Gospel that inspires you.

Wednesday

READINGS: Is 50:4–9 / Ps 69:8–10, 21–22, 31 and 33–34 / Mt 26:14–25

> "Woe to that man by whom the Son of Man is betrayed.
> It would be better for that man if he had never been
> born."
>
> —Matthew 26:24

JUDAS IS A COMPLEX FIGURE, simultaneously invoking hatred and pity. In the struggle to understand Judas, some movies and writers have attempted to portray his betrayal of Jesus in a compassionate light. He is sometimes depicted as a revolutionary who simply desired to bring about Jesus' reign and whose plan went terribly wrong. Others portray him as a man who just wanted the authorities to accept Jesus' mission, and thought that surely this would happen if only Jesus were given a fair hearing. However, Jesus' judgment of Judas' actions in today's Gospel is less than sympathetic. To hear the Son of God say, "It would be better for that man if he had never been born" should cause us to shudder in abject fear.

Clearly, Jesus thought that Judas' actions were inexcusable. In order to understand the events following the Last Supper, we too must comprehend the chilling evil behind Judas' act. Judas knew Jesus, saw his miracles, received his love, embraced him, and ate at the same table. Nevertheless, he chose to welcome evil into his heart and to betray his beloved Master. Before his betrayal, Luke describes how "Satan entered into Judas . . ." (Lk 22:3). Like Judas, countless Christians who have known Jesus well, gone to church, and proclaimed their faith, still have fallen into truly disturbing evil acts. Judas' shocking betrayal is an unsettling reminder to all Christians that we too can betray Jesus when we allow evil into our lives.

Judas gave into the spirit of the devil when he chose to believe that he knew better than Jesus. However, Judas' greatest mistake was not his act of prideful betrayal. Peter, the Rock, denied Jesus. And like Peter, Judas also admitted that he had sinned. After Jesus was condemned, he declared, "I have sinned in betraying innocent blood" (Mt 27:4). However, Judas did not do one thing that Peter did: trust in God's mercy. Judas' greatest mistake was his lack of faith in the inextinguishable mercy of God. In despair, Judas "departed and went off and hanged himself" (Mt 27:5). Judas' suicide does not necessarily mean that he went to hell. The Church reserves judgment on the eternal destination of all souls except canonized saints. For those who trust in the mercy of God, Judas' eternal fate remains a mystery. However, we can know for certain that if Judas were to have asked for Jesus' forgiveness even with his dying breath, he would have been forgiven.

As we enter the Triduum, the Church gives us this reading as a sobering warning to all earnest Christians. We are warned not only to avoid the influence of evil in our lives but also to take seriously the mercy of the Lord. Jesus lived, died, and rose to cancel our penalty for sin. However, the focal point of our Savior's actions is not our sins but the abundant, overflowing mercy of God. Every time we fall into temptation, even the greatest of evils, God's Merciful Life is ready to flow into our hearts, wash our souls clean, and give us a new start. The thought of our death is a reminder to continually accept God's mercy every day. Judas' greatest mistake was not to trust in this Mercy that was ready to forgive, to forget, and to help him to start anew. Let us not make this same mistake.

Examen and Intercessory Prayer

Review your day (see the Memento Mori Daily Examen, p. 8).

Pray a Hail Mary for the repose of the souls of those who have committed suicide. Entrust them and their families to the loving embrace of our Blessed Mother and to the mercy of the Lord.

> Oh, Mercy, who proceeds from your Eternal Father, the Divinity who governs with your power the whole world, by you were we created, in you were we recreated in the Blood of your Son. Your Mercy preserves us, your Mercy caused your Son to do battle for us, hanging by

his arms on the wood of the Cross, life and death battling together. Life confounded the death of our sin, and the death of our sin destroyed the bodily life of the Immaculate Lamb. Which one was finally conquered? Death! By what means? Mercy! Your Mercy gives light and life, by which your clemency is known in all your creatures, both the just and the unjust. In the height of heaven your mercy shines, that is, in your saints. If I turn to the earth, it abounds with your mercy. . . . By mercy you have washed us in the Blood, and by mercy you wish to converse with your creatures. Oh, Loving Madman! Was it not enough for you to become Incarnate, that you must also die? . . . Oh, Divine Mercy! My heart suffocates when thinking of you, for every way I turn in my thought, I find nothing but mercy. Oh, Eternal Father! Forgive my ignorance, that I presume to chatter in this way to you, but the love of your Mercy will be my excuse before the Face of your loving kindness.

— Saint Catherine of Siena, *The Dialogue*

Journaling and Prayer

Remember a time when you succumbed to great temptation. Did you seek forgiveness? Speak to God and ask for his forgiveness and plan to go to confession if you have not already. Now, remember a time when, through the grace of God, you overcame temptation. Ask God to help you to avoid temptation in the future.

Write a prayer to Jesus asking for his grace to avoid temptation and to follow his example.

Holy Thursday

READINGS: Ex 12:1–8, 11–14 / Ps 116:12–13, 15–16, 17–18 / 1 Cor 11:23–26 /
Jn 13:1–15

"Do you realize what I have done for you?"

—John 13:12

AFTER JESUS WASHES THE disciples' feet he asks a simple question that echoes through the centuries: *"Do you realize what I have done for you?"* Do we realize what Jesus has done for us? Not just when, like a slave, he descended to wash the feet of his disciples hours before he would die a slave's death on a Cross. But do we realize how Jesus' entire life was a descent? He "emptied himself, taking the form of a slave, coming in human likeness" (Phil 2:7). God became human. There is no greater descent, no greater act of service.

Jesus, the God who became a slave, wants us to follow in his footsteps. *"As I have done for you, you should also do"* (Jn 13:15). The problem, however, is that no one wants to be a slave. Upon hearing just the word, our hearts viscerally respond with immediate rebellion. Enamored of our freedom and blinded to reality, we fail to recognize that we are already slaves: "Everyone who commits sin is a slave of sin" (Jn 8:34). Basically, we have two choices. Saint Paul tells us we can either be slaves of "sin, which leads to death, or of obedience, which leads to righteousness" (Rom 6:16). When we run from Jesus' invitation to descend, we instead choose to enslave ourselves to death.

Death or righteousness: it's our choice. Jesus died in order to break the chains of slavery that bound us so that we might choose to live as children of God. Through Jesus' descent in his life, death, and resurrection, we have been given the opportunity to break free from the slavery of sin. In Baptism, we descend with Jesus into his death. From the waters of righteousness, we rise no longer slaves but adopted children of God. Thus, when Jesus asks, *"Do you realize what I have done for you?"* it is not a rhetorical question. He is looking for evidence that we realize what he has done. If we truly realize what he has done for us then we will eagerly descend to serve others and to serve God. And from this humble descent we can be sure that we will rise to new life.

Examen and Intercessory Prayer

Review your day (see the Memento Mori Daily Examen, p. 8).

Modern-day slavery happens in our own country and all over the world. Pray a Hail Mary for justice, freedom, and consolation for all people who are trafficked and enslaved.

> From my childhood I did not believe in the living God, but remained in death and unbelief until I was severely chastised. And, in truth, I have been humbled by hunger and nakedness; and even now I did not come to Ireland of my own will until I was nearly worn out. But this proved a blessing to me, for I was thus corrected by the Lord, and he made me fit to be today what was once far from my thoughts, so that I should care for the salvation of others. . . . For I am truly a debtor to God, who has given me so much grace that through me many people have been born again to God. . . .

> Behold how in Ireland they who never had the knowledge of God, and until now only worshipped unclean idols, have recently become the people of the Lord, and are called the sons of God. . . . But I confess to my Lord, and do not blush before him, because I tell the truth, that from the time I knew him in my youth the love of God and his fear increased within me, and until now, by the favor of the Lord, I have kept the faith. . . . I daily expect either death, or treachery, or slavery, or an occasion of some kind or another. But I fear none of these things, relying on the heavenly promise; for I have cast myself into the hands of the omnipotent God. . . .

> Behold, now I commend my soul to my most faithful God, whose mission I perform, notwithstanding my unworthiness; but because he does not accept persons, and has chosen me for this office, to be one of the least of his ministers. "What shall I render to him for all the things that he hath rendered to me?" But what

shall I say or promise to my Lord? For I see nothing unless he gives himself to me; but he searches the heart and soul, because I ardently desire and am ready that he should give me his cup to drink, as he has permitted others to do who have loved him. Wherefore may my Lord never permit me to lose his people whom he has gained in the ends of the earth. I pray God, therefore, that he may give me perseverance, and that he may vouchsafe to permit me to give him faithful testimony for my God until my death.

— Saint Patrick, *The Confession*

Journaling and Prayer

Sit with Jesus' question: "Do you realize what I have done for you?" Reflect on the gift of your life, the many blessings you have received, and on the people who love you. Spend time giving thanks to God.

Read the Canticle in Philippians 2:6–11, and spend time reflecting on the miracle of Jesus' descent and obedience until death and what it calls forth from you.

Good Friday

READINGS: Is 52:13–53:12 / Ps 31:2, 6, 12–13, 15–16, 17, 25 / Heb 4:14–16; 5:7–9 / Jn 18:1–19:42

So they took Jesus, and carrying the cross himself he went out to what is called the Place of the Skull, in Hebrew, Golgotha. There they crucified him.

—John 19:16–18

A HUSH FALLS OVER the world as God allows himself to be led to the Place of the Skull. As Jesus carries his Cross, the words he said to his disciples—"If anyone wishes to come after me, he must deny himself and take up his cross daily and follow me" (Lk 9:23)—take on a literal, ghastly meaning. Christ trudges up the hill, death looming ahead. He drags the heavy piece of wood to which he is about to be nailed. Drops of God-blood sprinkle the dusty road. Death is imminent for the Son of God, who could have easily avoided death.

Nevertheless, Jesus continues to plod ahead to face his death, to do the will of the Father.

Jesus' entire life was colored by this moment. Inevitable, violent death was the horizon that had shaped his entire life. It was imminent when he first gasped for air in Bethlehem. Then, the loving arms of Mary had placed him gently on the wood of the manger. Now, his arms thrust out like an infant's as the Roman soldiers throw him down on the wood of the Cross. Then, as a young boy, he had pounded nails into wood with Joseph. Now, nails are pounded through his hands into the wood of the Cross. Then, as a child, he had cried out in distress, and Mary had held him close to her breast. Now, Jesus cries out in pain as his mother stands powerless below.

Despite the fact that Jesus warned all of the disciples of his inevitable death, Mary was perhaps the only one who truly had prepared for it in her heart. She had known for a long time that her Son's blood would not remain forever inside his body to nourish and sustain his human existence. Simeon had told her that her Son was "a sign that will be contradicted" (Lk 2:34). She had seen the rejection Jesus had experienced. Mary had heard the harsh words and threats of bloodshed. She had always known and accepted that the violence that would strike her Son would also pierce her heart like a sword (see Lk 2:35).

Finally, that long-awaited day on Calvary had arrived. Drops of blood more precious than gold spatter Mary's face. But she does not notice. Mary is looking into the eyes of her Son, the incarnate God whose heart began to pump blood in her womb. Without a biological father, the blood coursing through Jesus' veins is wholly from her. Mary watched this blood course through Life's veins for over three decades. When Jesus changed water to wine, his heart pumped blood. When he healed, his heart pumped blood. When he spit on the ground and smeared mud on a blind man's eyes, his heart pumped blood. Now, as Jesus' heart pumps blood, it is poured out. Like a sacrificial lamb, his blood smears the wood of the Cross, the doorpost of all humanity (see Ex 12:17). Every drop of Life's blood gives life as it falls to the ground. Our God's blood ran down the wood of the Cross and into the earth—rain that would bring forth new life at the Place of the Skull.

Examen and Intercessory Prayer

Review your day (see the Memento Mori Daily Examen, p. 8).

Think of all those who do not realize the gift they have received through Christ's death. Pray a Hail Mary that all might accept the saving grace of Jesus Christ.

> [God the Father, speaking to Saint Catherine of Siena]: Inflamed with desire, my Son ran, with great eagerness, to the shameful death of the Cross. . . . He passed through like the true Captain and Knight that he was, whom I had placed on the battlefield to deliver you from the hands of the devil, so that you might be free, and drawn out of the most terrible slavery imaginable. And also to teach you his road, his doctrine, and his rule, so that you might open the Door of Me, Eternal Life, with the key of his precious Blood, shed with such

fire of love, with such hatred of your sins. It was as if the sweet and loving Word, My Son, had said to you: "Behold, I have made the road, and opened the door with My Blood." Do not then neglect to follow him by laying yourselves down to rest in self-love and ignorance of the road, presuming to choose to serve me in your own way, instead of in the way that I have made straight for you by means of my Truth, the Incarnate Word, and built up with his Blood. Rise up then, promptly, and follow him, for no one can reach me, the Father, if not by him; he is the Way and the Door by which you must enter into me.

— Saint Catherine of Siena, *The Dialogue*

Journaling and Prayer

Imagine yourself standing with the Blessed Mother beneath the Cross. Spend some time there and, as Saint Ignatius of Loyola urges in *The Spiritual Exercises*, "converse with Jesus. . . . Attach yourself to him with heart and mind so he may save you from eternal death." Remain in the scene for some time and then write down your prayer experience.

Draw some aspect of the crucifixion with a quote from today's Gospel that inspires you. Or write a prayer to Jesus, asking to be covered in his precious, saving blood.

Holy Saturday

Today's meditation follows a different format in order to better enter into this day's tomblike silence.

ON HOLY SATURDAY, WE WAIT in peaceful silence with the Blessed Mother, who expectantly awaited her Son's resurrection. While some celebrated Jesus' death and others despaired and doubted, Mary knew her Son would rise from the dead. As she knew her Son would die, she also knew he would rise. Mary believed and trusted that her Son would save all of humanity from death. She suffered as her Son suffered, but she also knew that death would not have the final say.

Today, we ask Mary to intercede to Jesus for us—just as she did for the couple at the Wedding of Cana (see Jn 2:1–12). At his mother's request, Jesus turned water into wine for a newly-married couple and their guests. Now, we ask Mary to beg Jesus to turn our doubts and lack of faith into the wine of faith and trust.

Mary, pray that we may trust as you did in the power of your Son to defeat death!

Examen and Intercessory Prayer

Review your day (see the Memento Mori Daily Examen, p. 8).

Read the following ancient homily for Holy Saturday and take some time for silent reflection.

What is happening? Today there is a great silence over the earth, a great silence, and stillness, a great silence because the King sleeps; the earth was in terror and was still, because God slept in the flesh and raised up those who were sleeping from the ages. God has died in the flesh, and the underworld has trembled.

Truly he goes to seek out our first parent like a lost sheep; he wishes to visit those who sit in darkness and in the shadow of death. He goes to free the prisoner Adam and his fellow-prisoner Eve from their pains, he who is God, and Adam's son.

The Lord goes in to them holding his victorious weapon, his Cross. When Adam, the first created man, sees him, he strikes his breast in terror and calls out to all: "My Lord be with you all."

And Christ in reply says to Adam: "And with your spirit." And grasping his hand he raises him up, saying: "Awake, O sleeper, and arise from the dead, and Christ shall give you light."

"I am your God, who for your sake became your son, who for you and your descendants now speak and command with authority those in prison: Come forth, and those in darkness: Have light, and those who sleep: Rise.

"I command you: Awake, sleeper, I have not made you to be held a prisoner in the underworld. Arise from the dead; I am the life of the dead. Arise, O man, work of my hands, arise, you who were fashioned in my image. Rise, let us go hence; for you in me and I in you, together we are one undivided person.

"For you, I your God became your son; for you, I the Master took on your form; that of slave; for you, I who am above the heavens came on earth and under the earth; for you, man, I became as a man without help, free among the dead; for you, who left a garden, I was handed over to Jews from a garden and crucified in a garden.

"Look at the spittle on my face, which I received because of you, in order to restore you to that first divine inbreathing at creation. See the blows on my cheeks, which I accepted in order to refashion your distorted form to my own image.

"See the scourging of my back, which I accepted in order to disperse the load of your sins which was laid upon your back. See my hands nailed to the tree for a good purpose, for you, who stretched out your hand to the tree for an evil one.

"I slept on the Cross and a sword pierced my side, for you, who slept in paradise and brought forth Eve from your side. My side healed the pain of your side; my sleep will release you from your sleep in Hades; my sword has checked the sword which was turned against you.

"But arise, let us go hence. The enemy brought you out of the land of paradise; I will reinstate you, no longer in paradise, but on the throne of heaven. I denied you the tree of life, which was a figure, but now I myself am united to you, I who am life. I posted the cherubim to guard you as they would slaves; now I make the cherubim worship you as they would God.

"The cherubim throne has been prepared, the bearers are ready and waiting, the bridal chamber is in order, the food is provided, the everlasting houses and rooms are in readiness; the treasures of good things have been opened; the kingdom of heaven has been prepared before the ages."

Vigil Gospel
    Year A: Mt 28:1–10; *Year B:* Mk 16:1–7; *Year C:* Lk 24:1–12

Easter Sunday

READINGS: Acts 10:34, 37–43 / Ps 118:1–2, 16–17, 22–23 / Col 3:1–4 or 1 Cor 5:6–8 / Jn 20:1–9

> On the first day of the week, Mary of Magdala came to the tomb early in the morning, while it was still dark, and saw the stone removed from the tomb.
>
> —John 20:1

ON THE MORNING AFTER THE SABBATH, just as sunlight broke open the darkness, Mary Magdalene quietly slipped out of the house to go to the tomb. The other Gospel writers mention that she was accompanied by other women to the tomb that morning. But John, perhaps in a nod to her singular role in the ensuing events, mentions only Mary Magdalene. As a known disciple of Jesus, she knew that she was putting her life in danger in order to be with her Lord. But Mary wanted to be near Jesus, even if it endangered her own life, and even if all that was left of Jesus was his dead body.

Mary Magdalene, whom tradition names the "Apostle to the Apostles," was one of the few who remained faithful to Jesus as he endured a brutal death. She stayed with the Blessed Mother and John at the foot of the Cross on Good Friday. Amidst so much betrayal, cowardice, and fear from Jesus' other followers, Mary was steadfast. She continued to act in faithful love when she returned to the tomb to anoint Jesus—the Messiah, the Anointed—one last time. However, even in her great faithfulness, she did not foresee the stunning reality that awaited her. She believed she was going to see a lifeless corpse. When she came upon the stone that was rolled away, she still assumed that the body of Jesus had been stolen (see Jn 20:2). Even Mary, the brave sentinel of the dawn, could not fathom the astonishing power of God.

For centuries, Mary Magdalene has been depicted in religious art as a young woman meditatively gazing at a skull. Assumed to have been a repentant harlot, the skull was a symbol of Mary's life of penance and conversion. While these assumptions about her past are now questioned by scholars, the skull remains an appropriate symbol to associate with this exemplary saint. Unlike the other disciples who ran away during Jesus' passion, Mary stared death in the face. All she saw was death as finality, an abyss of darkness—but still she stayed at the foot of the Cross and stared death down. After Jesus died, she did not remain in fear with the other Apostles behind locked doors. Instead, in the early hours of the morning, she went out and wept in sadness outside of the tomb. Saint Augustine once wrote, "Where is death?

Seek it in Christ, for it exists no longer; but it did exist and now it is dead. O Life, O Death of death!" Mary thought that death was the end, but nevertheless she sought it in Christ. When Jesus appeared to her, he shook her out of her sadness and fragmented understanding by simply saying her name, "Mary!" (Jn 20:16). While Mary forlornly but bravely stood over the chasm of death, Jesus rescued her and helped her to see that death was no longer an abyss but a shining doorway.

Mary Magdalene is the model par excellence for those who engage in the practice of remembering one's death. Although she could not comprehend or foresee God's glorious plan for death's end, she remained loyal to Jesus. She sought death in Christ. Consoled and fortified merely by her resilient love for Christ, even in death, Mary chose to simply reflect on the darkness. As she gazed upon the dark skull of death, she was amazed to find the light of Christ shining in it. As we too gaze on the intimidating skull of death, may we share in Mary Magdalene's joy at finding in death the dazzling light of Christ.

Examen and Intercessory Prayer

Review your day (see the Memento Mori Daily Examen, p. 8).

Pray a Hail Mary for all readers of this book, including yourself. Pray that the Holy Spirit will fill everyone's hearts with the inspiration to radically and wholeheartedly follow Jesus.

Devout and God-loving people, enjoy this beautiful and radiant festival. Wise people—come and share joy with your Lord. You who have labored in fasting, receive your deserved reward. You who have labored from the first hour, come to the festival now! You who came at the third hour, rejoice! You who lingered until the sixth hour, celebrate! You who came at the ninth hour, do not be sad! You who managed to come only at the eleventh hour, do not be dismayed by your lateness. No one will be deprived of heavenly joy. For our Lord is generous. He welcomes those who come last in the same way as those who come first. He is grateful to the first and rejoices in the last. He consoles those who came at the last hour, as if they had labored from the first hour. He gives to everyone: those who labored and those who wanted to labor. He receives the service and kisses the intention. He values the deed and praises the desire.

All of you enter into the joy of the Lord: First and last, receive the reward! Wealthy and poor, rejoice with one another! Diligent and lazy, celebrate the festival! Those who have fasted and those who have not—be glad together. The feast is abundant, eat your fill! All of you enjoy the wealthy banquet of the faith and mercy of God. Let no one go away hungry or offended. Let no one be sad about their poverty, for the kingdom is now here for everyone. Let no one weep over their sins, for forgiveness for all has burst with light from the grave. Let no one be afraid of death, for the death of Jesus has freed us all. Embraced by death, he subdued death. Having descended into hell, he took hell captive. He embittered it when it tasted of his flesh. Isaiah prophesied: "Hell was troubled, having met you in the underworld!" Hell was in mourning, for it was abolished! Hell was distressed, for it was condemned! Hell was impoverished, for it was deposed! Hell was destroyed, for it was bound! It took on the body and touched God. It took on the earth and met heaven. It took what it saw and fell to where it did not expect! Death! Where is your sting? Hell! Where is your victory? Christ is risen, and you are brought down. Christ is risen, and the demons have fallen. Christ is risen, and the angels rejoice. Christ is risen, and life triumphs. Christ is risen, and there are no dead in the grave. Christ has risen from the dead, become the firstborn of those who sleep and set into motion the resurrection of all. To him be glory now and forever. Amen!

—Saint John Chrysostom, *Paschal Homily*

Journaling and Prayer

Read John 20:1–18. Imagine that you are Mary Magdalene, weeping outside of Jesus' tomb. Why are you despairing? What is going through your mind? Hear Jesus say your name. What else does he say to you? Spend some time imagining this scene and praying with it.

Draw the stone rolled away or some other symbol of the resurrection. Or write a prayer of gratitude to Jesus for the gift of eternal life.

Christ, Triumphing over Sin and Death, Peter Paul Ruebens.

I will overcome the Evil One
through your forgiveness,
O All-Merciful;
and I shall overcome death
through Your Resurrection,
O All-Life-giver!

—Saint Ephrem the Syrian,
Nisibene Hymns, no. 52